the knitted
Odd-bod
Bunch

the knitted Odd-bod Bunch

35 unique and quirky knitted creatures

Donna Wilson

CICO BOOKS

LONDON NEW YORK

Published in 2009 by Cico Books
an imprint of Ryland Peters & Small Ltd
20–21 Jockey's Fields
London WC1R 4BW

www.cicobooks.co.uk

10 9 8 7 6 5 4 3 2

A CIP catalogue record for this book is available
from the British Library.

ISBN: 978-1-906525-41-5

Printed in China

Editor Kate Haxell
Designer Luis Peral-Aranda
Photographer Geoff Dann
Stylist Donna Wilson
Illustrator Luise Roberts

Contents

Introduction

Inspired as they are by the everyday oddities of life, I like to think of each of my creations as a character in my very own wonderland, a place where scale and perception are there to be played with. I love the naïvety of children's drawings and the idea that everyone has their quirks. So Harry Hairy Head has a big head and small body, and he likes to groom his hairy head. Peggy Long Legs has extremely long legs, which keep growing as she gets older!

What will happen to you today in Donna's World? You could hang out with Humphrey Hare, pamper a poodle, escape to the woods with the Squirrel-Fox family or simply have a nibble on a giant, fat-free cupcake!

Especially for this book, my characters have been interpreted into hand knit patterns. This has enabled me to explore knitting techniques that lend themselves to each character, techniques that have given them each a new twist that I love.

Novice knitters will find projects such as Sleepy Pom (page 36) and Percival Long Dog (page 91) very achievable as they just involve a bit of shaping – see instructions for that on pages 118–119 if you need them. Sock knitters will love Oscar Dog (page 41), Fifi Flamingo (page 79) and Stick Snail (page 51), who are some of the creatures that are knitted in the round. If you like cable knitting, then try your hand at Vanessa Hare (page 60), while bead-knitting fans will want to make Deirdre Dragonfly (page 100). For colour enthusiasts there are Fair Isle designs including Mitten Kitten (page 69) and Aggie Bear (page 44), plus simpler striped knits, such as Evel Bee (page 74) and Ginge Marmalade (page 13).

I hope you like my creatures – maybe they will remind you of some of your friends! Enjoy knitting them and feel free to send a picture of your new knitted friend to info@donnawilson.com, where I will add some of them to my picture gallery.

Donna Wilson

Charlie Monkey is always hanging around! He once climbed the Eiffel Tower without ropes! His hobbies are eating high-energy food and drinking banana milkshakes, going to the gym to strengthen his upper body muscles and talking to himself — especially when concentrating.

Charlie Monkey

pattern

Note: two strands of Rowan Scottish Tweed are used together throughout to even out the variable weight of the tweed yarn.

FRONT and BACK (both alike)
First leg
*Using the thumb method and A, cast on 5 sts.
Row 1 (RS): Knit.
Row 2: P1, M1L, p3, M1R, p1. (7 sts)
Row 3: K1, M1R, k5, M1L, k1. (9 sts)
Row 4: P1, M1L, p7, M1R, p1. (11 sts)
Row 5: Knit.
Row 6: Purl.
Starting with a k row, work 74 rows st st.*
Cut yarn and put sts onto stitch holder.

Second leg
Work as for First Leg from * to *.
Leave sts on needle and do not cut yarn.

Join legs
Row 81: Knit across 11 sts on needles, cast on 3 sts using the backward loop method, knit across 11 sts from stitch holder. (25 sts)
Row 82: P10, p2tog, p1, p2togtbl, p10. (23 sts)

Body
Starting with a k row, work 62 rows st st.

Shape cheeks
Row 145: K1, M1R, k21, M1L, k1. (25 sts)
Row 146: P1, M1L, p23, M1R, p1. (27 sts)
Row 147: K1, M1R, k25, M1L, k1. (29 sts)
Row 148: Purl.

Row 149: Knit.
Row 150: Purl.
Row 151: K1, skpo, k23, k2tog, k1. (27 sts)
Row 152: P1, p2tog, p21, p2togtbl, p1. (25 sts)
Row 153: K1, skpo, k19, k2tog, k1. (23 sts)
Starting with a p row, work 11 rows st st.
Row 165: K1, skpo, k17, k2tog, k1. (21 sts)
Row 166: Purl.
Row 167: K1, skpo, k15, k2tog, k1. (19 sts)
Row 168: Purl.
Row 169: K1, skpo, k13, k2tog, k1. (17 sts)
Row 170: P1, p2tog, p11, p2togtbl, p1. (15 sts)
Cast off.

ARMS (make two)
Using the thumb method and A, cast on 13 sts.
Row 1: Knit.
Row 2: Purl.
Starting with a k row, work 86 rows st st.
Row 89: [K2, k2tog] three times, k1. (10 sts)
Row 90: Purl.
Row 91: [K1, k2tog] three times, k1. (7 sts)
Row 92: [P2tog] three times, k1. (4 sts)
Cut yarn leaving a long tail. Pass yarn through rem 4 sts, pull up tight and secure end.

TAIL
Work as for Arms.

NOSE

Using the thumb method and B, cast on
7 sts.

Row 1: Knit.

Row 2: P1, M1L, p5, M1R, p1. (9 sts)

Row 3: K1, M1R, k7, M1L, k1. (11 sts)

Row 4: Purl.

Row 5: K1, M1R, k9, M1L, k1. (13 sts)
Starting with a p row, work 3 rows st st.

Row 9: K1, M1R, k11, M1L, k1. (15 sts)

Row 10: P1, M1L, p13, M1R, p1. (17 sts)

Row 11: Knit.

Row 12: P1, M1L, p15, M1R, p1. (19 sts)
Starting with a k row, work 3 rows st st.

Row 16: P1, p2tog, p13, p2togtbl, p1.
(17 sts)

Row 17: Knit.

Row 18: P1, p2tog, p11, p2togtbl, p1.
(15 sts)

Row 19: K1, skpo, k9, k2tog, k1. (13 sts)
Starting with a p row, work 3 rows st st.

Row 23: K1, skpo, k7, k2tog, k1. (11 sts)

Row 24: Purl.

Row 25: K1, skpo, k5, k2tog, k1. (9 sts)

Row 26: P1, p2tog, p3, p2togtbl, p1. (7 sts)
Cast off.

TO MAKE UP

Press pieces gently following directions on
the ball band.
Note that the arms and tail are not stuffed.
Pin nose to centre of face, following
photograph for position. Thread a
tapestry needle with yarn B and using
mattress stitch, sew around edge of nose
to attach it to face. Before completing
sewing, insert toy filling in nose.
Pin arms to edges of front body approx.
15cm from top of head. Using mattress
stitch, sew body pieces together around
outer edges, catching arms into seam,
weaving loose ends into the seam wherever
possible and leaving a small opening. Insert
toy filling and sew opening closed.
Sew the tail to the back, centred just above
the legs.

Embroider as follows:
The face: for each eye, using black tapestry
wool and backstitch, embroider an oval with
a vertical line either side of the iris area. Fill
in the irises with satin stitch in blue and the
areas on either side with satin stitch in
white; for the eyebrows, using black and
backstitch, embroider a short line above each
eye; for the mouth, using black and backstitch,
embroider a horizontal line on the nose. See
also page 124.

Harry is one of a kind: he eats fluff for lunch and always loves being brushed and groomed. He is well known for his hairy head and sometimes makes people around him sneeze.

Harry Hairy Head

pattern

Note: two strands of Kid Classic are used together for Head, one from each ball.

FRONT and BACK BODY (both alike)
First leg
*Using 2.50mm needles, the cable method and A, cast on 10 sts.
Row 1 (RS): Knit.
Row 2: Purl.
Row 3: K2, M1R, k to last 2 sts, M1L, k2. (12 sts)
Row 4: Purl.
Rep rows 3–4 once more. (14 sts)
Row 7: Knit.
Row 8: Purl.*
Cut yarn, put sts onto stitch holder.

Second leg
Work as for First Leg from * to *.
Leave sts on needle and do not cut yarn.

Join legs
Knit across 14 sts on needle, cast on 10 sts, knit across 14 sts from stitch holder. (38 sts)

Body
Starting with a p row, work 19 rows st st,

Shape arms
Next row: K2, M1R, k to last 2 sts, M1L, k2. (40 sts)
Next row: Purl.
Rep last 2 rows once more. (42 sts)
Next row: Knit.
Next row: Cast on 8 sts, p to end. (50 sts)
Next row: Cast on 8 sts, k to end. (58 sts)
Next row: Purl.

Next row: K2, M1R, k to last 2 sts, M1L, k2. (60 sts)
Next row: Purl.
Rep last 2 rows once more. (62 sts)
Next row: Knit.
Next row: Purl.
Rep last 2 rows once more.
Next row: K2, skpo, k to last 4 sts, k2tog, k2. (60 sts)
Next row: Purl.
Rep last 2 rows once more. (58 sts)
Next row: Knit.
Next row: Cast off 10 sts, p to end. (48 sts)
Next row: Cast off 10 sts, k to end. (38 sts)
Next row: Purl.
Next row: Knit.
Put sts onto holder.
Block and press both pieces on holders.

HEAD
With WS of one body piece facing and using two ends of B, purl 25 sts from holder onto first 4mm double-pointed needle. Purl rem 13 sts onto second double-pointed needle. With WS of second body piece facing, purl 13 sts onto second double-pointed needle, purl final 25 sts onto third double-pointed needle. (76 sts)
Keeping WS of body facing outwards, use fourth needle to work in the round.
Knit three rounds, thus establishing rev st st on RS of work, and cont work on WS of head.

Size
Completed creature measures approx. 38cm tall

Yarn suggestion
Fine-weight yarn (such as Rowan Cotton Glacé) 1 x 50g ball in A (green – Ivy 812)
Lightweight-Aran mohair yarn (such as Rowan Kid Classic) 2 x 50g balls in B (lilac – Lavender Ice 841)

Needles
Pair of 2.50mm knitting needles
Set of four double-pointed 4mm knitting needles

Extras
Two stitch holders
Two round markers
Tapestry needle
Washable toy filling
Oddments of black, green and white tapestry wool for embroidery

Tension
21 stiches and 30 rows to 10cm over rev st st using two ends of B and 4mm needles

Abbreviations
See page 126

Place round marker before first and 39th sts.
Next round: *K1, k2tog, k to 3 sts before marker, skpo, k1, rep from * once more. (72 sts)
Knit 1 round.
Rep last two rounds three more times. (60 sts)
Knit 7 rounds.
Next round: K to 1 st before marker, M1, k2, M1, k to end. (62 sts)

Knit 1 round.
Rep last 2 rounds once more. (64 sts)
Next round: K1, M1, k to 1 st before marker, M1, k2, M1, k to last st, M1, k1. (68 sts)
Knit 1 round.
Rep last 2 rounds once more. (72 sts)
Next round: K to 1 st before marker, M1, k2, M1, k to end. (74 sts)
Knit 1 round.
Rep last 2 rounds six more times. (86 sts)

Knit 9 rounds.
Next round: K2, k2tog, k to last 4 sts, skpo, k2. (84 sts)
Rep last round four more times. (76 sts)
Knit 1 round.
Next round: *K1, k2tog, k to 3 sts before marker, skpo, k1, rep from * once more. (72 sts)
Rep last 2 rounds nine more times. (36 sts)
Next round: *K1, k2tog, k to 3 sts before marker, skpo, k1, rep from * once more. (32 sts)
Rep last round four more times. (16 sts)
Rearrange sts so there are 8 sts on each of first and second needles.
Cast off all sts, casting off 1 st from each needle together.

TO MAKE UP
Weave in all loose ends.
Turn creature inside out so RS (rev st st) side of head is outermost. Roll up a cotton tea towel and place it inside head as a former, then steam head gently.
Using mattress stitch, sew body pieces together around outer edges from neck to underarm. Insert toy filling into head and arms through open legs, then sew up leg seams, inserting toy filling in legs as you sew seam.
Embroider as follows:
The face: for each eye, using black tapestry wool and backstitch, embroider an oval with a vertical line either side of the iris area. Fill in the irises with satin stitch in green and the areas on either side with satin stitch in white; for the eyebrows, using black and backstitch, embroider a line above each eye; for the mouth, using black and backstitch, embroider an oval opening and outline the teeth. Fill in the teeth with satin stitch in white. See also page 124.

Ginge Marmalade

Ginge is a pure-bred marmalade cat. During the day he doesn't do much apart from eat and sleep, but at night he gets up to all sorts of fun. He has held the record for singing on a tightrope while holding a pint of milk with his tail!

pattern

FRONT

First leg

*Using the thumb method and A, cast on
3 sts.

Row 1 (RS): Knit.

Row 2: P1, M1L, p1, M1R, p1. (5 sts)
Join in B.

Row 3: Using B, k1, M1R, k3, M1L, k1.
(7 sts)

Row 4: Using B, purl.
The last 4 rows form the st st stripe patt, rep
throughout. Strand the yarn not in use on
the WS up the right-hand edge. Work
shaping as follows:

Row 5: K1, M1R, k5, M1L, k1. (9 sts)
Starting with a p row, work 5 rows st st.*
Cut yarns and put sts onto stitch holder.

Second and third legs

Work as for First Leg.

Fourth leg

Work as for First Leg from * to *.
Leave sts on needle and do not cut yarns.

Join legs

Keeping the stripe patt correct:

Row 11: Knit across 9 sts of the Fourth Leg,
[cast on 2 sts using the backward loop
method, with RS facing, knit across 9 sts of
the next Leg on stitch holder] three times.
(42 sts)

Body

Row 12: P8, [p2togtbl, p2tog, p7] twice,
p2tog, p2togtbl, p8. (36 sts)
Starting with a k row, work 6 rows st st,
ending after 2 rows using A.

Row 19: Using B, k1, skpo, k to end.
(35 sts)
Starting with a p row, work 3 rows st st.

Row 23: Using B, k1, skpo, k to end.
(34 sts)

Row 24: Purl.

Row 25: Using A, k1, skpo, k to end. (33 sts)

Row 26: Purl.

Row 27: Using B, k1, skpo, k to end. (32 sts)

Row 28: Purl.

Row 29: Using A, k1, skpo, k to end. (31 sts)

Row 30: Purl.

Row 31: Using B, k1, skpo, k to end. (30 sts)

Row 28: Purl.

Row 29: Using A, k1, skpo, k to end. (29 sts)
Starting with a p row, work 3 rows st st.

Row 33: Using A, k1, skpo, k to end. (28 sts)
Starting with a p row, work 5 rows st st.

Row 39: Using B, k1, skpo, k to last 3 sts,
k2tog, k1. (26 sts)
Starting with a p row, work 7 rows st st.

Row 47: Using B, k1, skpo, k to end. (25 sts)
Starting with a p row, work 9 rows st st.

Row 57: Using A, k1, skpo, k to end. (24 sts)
Starting with a p row, work 9 rows st st,
ending after 2 rows using A.

Shape first ear

Row 67: K8 and turn.
Work on this set of 8 sts only and put the
rem sts on a stitch holder.

Row 68: P1, p2tog, p to end. (7 sts)

Row 69: K to last 3 sts, k2tog, k1. (6 sts)
Rep rows 68–69 twice more. (2 sts)
Cast off and cut yarns.

Shape second ear

Put the 16 sts from stitch holder onto
needle, with RS facing rejoin yarn.

Row 67: Cast off 8 sts, k to end. (8 sts).

Row 68: P to last 3 sts, p2togtbl, p1.
(7 sts)

Row 69: K1, skpo, k to end. (6 sts)
Rep rows 68–69 twice more. (2 sts)
Cast off and cut yarns.

BACK

Work as given for Front, reversing RS of work (to make a mirrored pair of pieces) by reading knit for purl and vice versa. See page 118 for reverse shaping tips.

TAIL

Using the thumb method and A, cast on 12 sts.

Row 1 (RS): Knit.

Row 2: Purl.

Join in B.

Row 3: Knit.

Row 4: Purl.

The last 4 rows form the st st stripe patt, rep throughout. Strand the yarn not in use on the WS up the right-hand edge.

Starting with a k row, work 112 rows in st st, ending after 2 rows using B.

Row 117: Using A, [k2, k2tog] three times. (9 sts)

Row 118: Using A, purl.

Cut A.

Row 119: Using B, [k1, k2tog] three times. (6 sts)

Row 120: Using B, [p2tog] three times. (3 sts)

Cut yarn leaving a long tail. Pass yarn through rem 3 sts, pull up tight and secure.

TO MAKE UP

Press pieces gently following directions on the ball band.

Note that the tail is not stuffed.

Using mattress stitch, sew row ends of tail together, leaving cast-on end open.

Position tail at the bottom of decrease edge on front body. Using mattress stitch, sew body pieces together around the outer edge, catching tail into seam, weaving loose ends into the seam wherever possible and leaving a small opening. Insert toy filling and sew opening closed.

Embroider as follows:

The face: for each eye, using black tapestry wool and backstitch, embroider an oval with a vertical line either side of the iris area. Fill in the irises with satin stitch in green and the areas on either side with satin stitch in white; for the nose and mouth, using black and backstitch, embroider an inverted triangle with a vertical line descending from the apex to touch the top of a second triangle; for the whiskers, using white make fringe loops (as you would for the ends of a scarf) under stitches on each cheek. See also page 124.

Neerg's favourite food is grass. He used to be a white bunny, but since he started eating grass his fur has changed colour permanently.

Neerg Green Bunny

pattern

FRONT and BACK (both alike)

First leg

*Using the thumb method and A, cast on 5 sts.

Row 1 (WS): Purl.

Row 2: K1, M1R, k3, M1L, k1. (7 sts)

Row 3: P1 [k1, yarn forward between the needles, sl1, yarn back between the needles] rep to last 2 sts, k1, p1.

Row 4: Knit.

Row 5: As row 3.

Rows 6–7: Rep rows 4–5.

Row 8: K1, M1R, k5, M1L, k1. (9 sts)

Row 9: P1 [yarn forward between the needles, sl1, yarn back between the needles k1] rep to last 2 sts, yarn forward between the needles, sl1, p1.

Row 10: Knit.

Row 11: As row 9.*

Cut yarn and put sts onto stitch holder.

Second leg

Work as for First Leg from * to *.
Cut yarn and leave sts on needle.

Join legs

Join in B.

Row 12 (RS): Knit across 9 sts on needle, cast on 20 sts using the backward loop method, knit across 9 sts from stitch holder. (38 sts)

Row 13: P8, p2tog, p18, p2togtbl, p8. (36 sts)

Row 14: Knit.

Row 15: Purl.

Starting with a k row, work 20 rows st st.

Shape arms

Row 36: K1, M1R, k to last st, M1L, k1. (38 sts)

Row 37: P1, M1L, p to last st, M1R, p1. (40 sts)

Rep rows 36–37 twice more. (48 sts)

Starting with a k row, work 2 rows st st.

Row 44: K1, skpo, k to last 3 sts, k2tog, k1. (46 sts)

Row 45: P1, p2tog, p to last 3 sts, p2togtbl, p1. (44 sts)

Rep rows 44–45 twice more. (36 sts)

Starting with a k row, work 10 rows st st.

Shape first ear

Row 60: K9 and turn.

Work on this set of 9 sts only and put the rem stitches onto a stitch holder.

**Starting with a p row, work 15 rows st st.

Row 76: K1, skpo, k3, k2tog, k1. (7 sts)

Row 77: Purl.

Cast off as follows: k1, skpo, pass the first st loop on the right-hand needle over the second, k1, pass the first st loop on the right-hand needle over the second, k2tog, pass the first st loop on the right-hand needle over the second, k1, pass the first st loop on the right-hand needle over the second.

Fasten off.**

Shape second ear

Put next 9 sts on stitch holder onto needle, rejoin yarn with RS facing, k9, turn,
Rep from ** to **.

Shape third ear

Work as for Second Ear.

Shape fourth ear

Work as for Second Ear.

Size

Completed creature measures approx. 20cm tall

Yarn suggestion

Lightweight yarn (such as Rowan Wool Cotton) small amount in A (green – Elf 946) and 1 x 50g ball in B (acid green – Citron 901)

Fine-weight yarn (such as Rowan Pure Wool 4 ply) small amount in C (cream – Snow 412)

Needles

Pair of 3.25mm knitting needles

Extras

One stitch holder

Tapestry needle

Washable toy filling

Oddments of black, green, white and pink tapestry wool for embroidery

Tension

26 stitches and 36 rows to 10cm over st st using 3.25mm needles

Abbreviations

See page 126

TO MAKE UP

Press pieces gently following directions on the ball band.

Using mattress stitch, sew body pieces together around the outer edges, leaving a small opening. Insert toy filling and sew opening closed.

Using C, make a small pom-pom and attach to back of the body.

Embroider as follows:

The face: for each eye, using black tapestry wool and backstitch, embroider an oval with a vertical line either side of the iris area. Fill in the irises with satin stitch in green and the areas on either side with satin stitch in white; for each mouth, using pink, embroider a cross. See also page 124.

Size
Completed creature measures approx.
18cm tall

Yarn suggestion
Fine-weight yarn (such as Rowan
Cotton Glacé) 1 x 50g ball in
A (sand – Ochre 833) and 1 ball in
B (red – Poppy 741)

Needles
Pair of 3mm knitting needles
Set of four double-pointed 3mm
knitting needles

Extras
Tapestry needle
Washable toy filling
Oddments of black, brown, white and
red tapestry wool for embroidery

Tension
28 stitches and 42 rows to 10cm over
st st using 3mm needles

Abbreviations
See page 126

Stripy Head is one of the smallest in the world of the creatures. He loves hiding from people and popping out in the most unexpected places. He is fond of jam sandwiches and dislikes seafood.

Stripy Head

pattern

ARMS (make four)
Using 3mm needles, the thumb method and
A, cast on 5 sts.
Row 1 (RS): Using A, knit.
Row 2: Using A, purl.
Join in B.
Row 3: Using B, knit.
Row 4: Using B, purl.
Cut A and B 10cm from last st on needle,
put sts onto a double-pointed needle.

FRONT and BACK BODY (both alike)
First leg
Using 3mm needles, the thumb method and
A, cast on 5 sts.
Row 1 (RS): Using A, knit.
Row 2: Using A, purl.
Join in B.
Row 3: Using B, k to last st, M1L, k1. (6 sts)
Row 4: Using B, purl.
The last 4 rows form the stripe st st patt,
rep throughout. Strand the yarn not in use
on the WS up the right-hand edge. Work
as follows:
Starting with a k row, work 4 rows st st.

Cut A and B 10cm from last st on needle,
put sts onto a double-pointed needle.
Second leg
Using 3mm needles, the thumb method and
A, cast on 5 sts.
Row 1 (RS): Using A, knit.
Row 2: Using A, purl.
Join in B.
Row 3: Using B, k1, M1R, k to end. (6 sts)
Row 4: Using B, purl.
Starting with a k row, work 4 rows in stripe
st st patt.
Do not cut yarn.

Join legs
Keeping the stripe patt correct.
Row 9: Using A, knit across 6 sts on needle,
cast on 4 sts using the backward loop
method, with RS facing, knit across 6 sts
from double-pointed needle. (16 sts)
Row 10: Using A, p5, p2tog, p2, p2togtbl,
p5. (14 sts)
Row 11: Using B, knit.
Row 12: Using B, p1, p2tog, p to last 3 sts,
p2togtbl, p1. (12 sts)

Starting with a k row, work 3 rows in stripe
st st patt.
Row 16: Using B, p1, p2tog, p to last 3 sts,
p2togtbl, p1. (10 sts)
Starting with a k row, work 8 rows in stripe
st st patt.
Cut A and B 10cm from last st on needle.

Join in arms
Row 25: Using A and RS facing, k5 sts of
one arm piece, cast on 3 sts using the
backward loop method, k10 sts of the body
section, cast on 3 sts using the backward
loop method, k5 sts of a second arm piece.
(26 sts)
Row 26: Using A, p1, [p2tog, p1] twice,
p2togtbl, p8, p2tog, [p1, p2togtbl] twice,
p1. (20 sts).
Row 27: Using B, knit.
Row 28: Using B, p1, p2tog, p to last 3 sts,
p2togtbl, p1. (18 sts)
Row 29: Using A, knit.
Row 30: Using A, p1, p2tog, p to last 3 sts,
p2togtbl, p1. (16 sts)
Rep rows 27–30 once more. (12 sts)
Cut A and B 10cm from last st on needle,
put sts onto a double-pointed needle.

HEAD
Select one Front/Back piece as the Back.
Starting with this piece RS facing, arrange
the stitches on three double-pointed needles
as follows:
Slip the left 6 sts from the Back and the
following 2 sts from the Front onto a third
needle, slip 8 sts from the Front onto a
fourth needle and slip the rem 2 sts on the
front needle onto the back needle. Place a
round marker at the centre back. (8 sts on
each needle)
Join in B at the centre back.
Rounds 1–2: Using B, knit.
Join in A, Cont to work in stripe patt,
twisting the yarns together at each colour
change and stranding the colour not in use
on the WS.
Rounds 3–4: Using A, knit.
Rep rounds 1–2 once more.
Round 7: Using A, knit.
Round 8: Using A, k1, M1R, k6, M1L, k1 on
each needle. (10 sts on each needle)
Knit 3 rounds in stripe patt set.
Round 12: Using A, k1, M1R, k8, M1L, k1
on each needle. (12 sts on each needle)
Knit 3 rounds in stripe patt set.
Round 16: Using A, k1, M1R, k10, M1L, k1
on each needle. (14 sts on each needle)
Knit 3 rounds in stripe patt set.
Round 20: Using A, k1, M1R, k12, M1L, k1
on each needle. (16 sts on each needle)
Knit 3 rounds in stripe patt set.
Round 24: Using A, k1, M1R, k14, M1L, k1
each needle. (18 sts on each needle)
Knit 19 rounds in stripe patt set.
Round 44: Using A, k1, skpo, k3, k2tog, k2,
skpo, k3, k2tog, k1 on each needle. (14 sts
on each needle)
Cut A and cont in B.
Round 45: K1, skpo, k1, k2tog, k2, skpo,
k1, k2tog, k1 on each needle. (10 sts on
each needle)

Round 46: K1, [skpo, k2tog] twice, k1 on
each needle. (6 sts on each needle)
Round 47: K1, skpo, k2tog, k1 on each
needle. (4 sts on each needle)
Round 48: K1, k2tog, k1 on each needle.
(3 sts on each needle)
Cut B 10cm from the last stitch on the
needle and thread into a tapestry needle.
Pass the tapestry needle through all the
stitches on the needles in the order they
would have been knitted, use the tip of the
needle to pull the yarn at the point just after
it has passed through the first stitch to draw
the stitches tight to the yarn, then pull the
yarn tight as it emerges through the last
stitch. Secure the end.

TO MAKE UP
Press pieces gently following directions on
the ball band.
Using mattress stitch, sew body pieces
together around the outer edges, weaving
loose ends into seam wherever possible and
leaving a small opening. Insert toy filling and
sew opening closed.
Embroider as follows:
The face: for each eye, using black tapestry
wool and backstitch, embroider an oval with
a vertical line either side of the iris area. Fill
in the irises with satin stitch in brown and
the areas on either side with satin stitch in
white; for the eyebrows, using black and
backstitch, embroider a short, slanting line
above each eye; for the mouth, using black
and backstitch, embroider a small oval and
fill this in with satin stitch in red. See also
page 124.

Beryl the Bold

Beryl is a dog-cat: she's definitely a dog, but traces of cat have been found in her ancestry. She always got teased at school for this, but now she's happy with who she is! She loves chocolate chip ice cream and going on short walks. She's sometimes a bit moody but always says sorry if she's snapped at anyone.

Size

Completed creature measures approx.
12cm tall

Yarn suggestion

Lightweight yarn (such as Rowan
Wool Cotton) 1 x 50g ball in
A (cream – Antique 900) and 1 ball in
B (light brown – Dream 929)

Needles

Pair of 3mm knitting needles

Extras

Two stitch holders or large safety pins

Tapestry needle

Washable toy filling

Oddments of black, green and white
tapestry wool for embroidery

1 x 20cm of pink craft felt

Small bell

Tension

23 stitches and 32 rows to 10cm over
st st using 3mm needles

Abbreviations

See page 126

pattern

FRONT

Back leg

Using the thumb method and A, cast on
3 sts.

Row 1 (RS): Knit.

Row 2: P1, M1L, p1, M1R, p1. (5 sts)

Row 3: Knit.

Row 4: Purl.

Rep rows 3–4 once more.

Row 7: Knit.

Row 8: P4, M1R, p1. (6 sts)

Cut yarn and put sts onto a stitch holder.

Second leg

Using the thumb method and A, cast
on 3 sts.

Row 1: Knit.

Row 2: P1, M1L, p1, M1R, p1. (5 sts)

Starting with a k row, work 5 rows st st.

Row 8: P1, M1L, p3, M1R, p1. (7 sts)

Cut yarn and put sts onto a stitch holder.

Third and fourth legs

Work as for Second Leg.

Join legs

Row 9: Cast on 17 sts, knit across 7 sts of
fourth leg, cast on 3 sts using the backward
loop method, with RS facing, knit across
7 sts of the third leg, cast on 18 sts using
the backward loop method, knit across 7 sts
of the second leg, cast on 3 sts using the
backward loop method, knit across 6 sts of
the back leg. (68 sts)

Shape body

Row 10: P5, p2tog, p1, p2togtbl, p5, p2tog,
p16, p2togtbl, p5, p2tog, p1, p2togtbl, p5,
p2tog, p16.
(61 sts)
Join in B.

Starting with a knit (RS) row and using a
separate length of yarn for each block of
colour, twisting the colours together on the
WS to avoid holes forming, work colour patt
from the chart. Work shaping as follows:

Row 11: K1, M1R, k to end. (62 sts)

Row 12: P to last st, M1R, p1. (63 sts)

Rows 13–18: Rep rows 11–12 three times.
(69 sts)

Row 19: K1, M1R, k to end. (70 sts)

Row 20: Purl.

Rows 21–26: Rep rows 19–20 three times.
(73 sts)

Row 27: Knit.

Row 28: Purl.

Row 29: K1, M1R, k to end. (74 sts)

Head

Row 30: P7, put the last 7 sts onto a stitch
holder, cast off 35 sts, p to end.

Work on this set of 32 sts only for the head.

Row 31: K to last 3 sts, k2tog, k1. (31 sts)

Row 32: P1, p2tog, p to end. (30 sts)

Row 33: K1, M1R, k to last 3 sts, k2tog, k1.
(30 sts)

Row 34: P1, p2tog, p to end. (29 sts)

Row 35: Knit.

Rows 36–39: Rep rows 34–35 twice. (27 sts)

Row 40: Purl.

Row 41: Knit.

Row 42: Purl.

Shape first ear

Row 43: K6, put the last 6 sts onto a stitch
holder, cast off 15 sts, k5.

Cut B and cont work using A.

Work on this set of 6 sts only for the first ear.

Row 44: P3, p2togtbl, p1. (5 sts)

Row 45: K1, skpo, k2. (4 sts)

Row 46: P1, p2togtbl, p1. (3 sts)

Cast off.

Shape second ear

Put sts on second stitch holder onto needle
and with WS facing rejoin A.

Row 44: P1, p2tog, p3. (5 sts)

Row 45: K2, k2tog, k1. (4 sts)

Row 46: P1, p2tog, p1. (3 sts)

Cast off.

Tail

Put sts on first stitch holder onto needle and
with the RS facing rejoin A.

Row 31: K1, skpo, k4. (6 sts)

Row 32: P3, p2togtbl, p1. (5 sts)

Cut A and join in B.

Row 33: Knit.

Row 34: P2, p2togtbl, p1. (4 sts)

Rows 35–39: Starting with a k row, work 5 rows st st.

Row 40: P2tog, p2togtbl. (2 sts)

Cast off.

BACK

Work as given for Front, reversing RS of work (to make a mirrored pair of pieces) by reading knit for purl and vice versa. See page 118 for reverse shaping tips.

TO MAKE UP

Press pieces gently following directions on the ball band.

Using mattress stitch; sew the body pieces together around the outer edges, weaving loose ends into seam wherever possible and leaving a small opening. Insert toy filling and sew opening closed.

Embroider as follows:

The face: for each eye, using black tapestry wool and backstitch, embroider an oval with a vertical line either side of the iris area. Fill in the irises with satin stitch in green and the areas on either side with satin stitch in white; for the nose, using black and satin stitch, embroider an inverted triangle with a vertical line of backstitch descending from the apex; for the mouth, using black and backstitch, embroider a circular opening and outline the teeth. Fill in the teeth with satin stitch in white. See also page 124.

Cut the felt to fit around Beryl's neck, sew on the bell and sew the ends of the collar together around her neck.

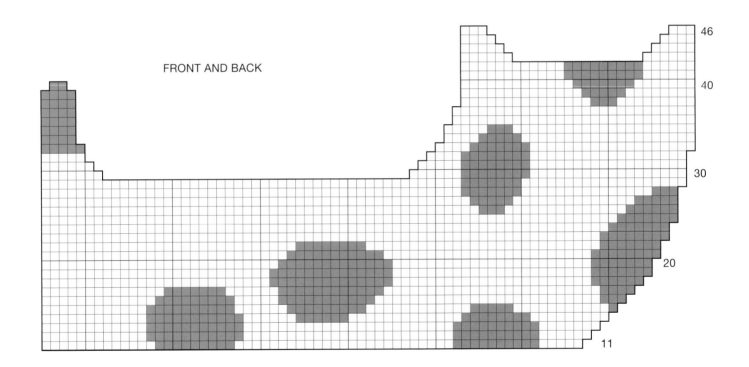

FRONT AND BACK

A

B

Tig is Beryl and Ginge's only child and is their pride and joy, Tig was named after her great-grandfather, Tigger, who was a very famous actor. She is small and cuddly and loves everything pink.

Little Tig

pattern

Note: one length of yarn A is used for the body with shorter lengths of yarn B worked together with yarn A for the spots as indicated on the chart.

FRONT

Front leg

*Using the thumb method and A, cast on 5 sts.

Row 1 (WS): Purl.

Row 2: K1, M1R, k3, M1L, k1. (7 sts)

Starting with a p row, work 3 rows st st.

Row 6: K1, M1R, k5, M1L, k1. (9 sts)

Starting with a p row, work 3 rows st st.

Row 10: K8, M1L, k1. (10 sts)

Row 11: Purl.*

Cut yarn and put sts onto stitch holder.

Back leg

Using A and B stranded together, work as for First Leg from * to *.

Leave sts on needle and do not cut yarn.

Join legs

Row 12: Using A and B stranded together, knit across 10 sts on needle, cast on 4 sts using the backward loop method, using A only and RS facing, knit across 10 sts from stitch holder, cast on 22 sts using the backward loop method. (46 sts)

Body

Row 13: P21, p2togtbl, p8, p2tog, using A and B together p2, p2togtbl, p9. (43 sts)

Starting with a knit (RS) row and using a separate length of B for each block of A and B colour indicated, work colour patt from the chart. Work shaping as follows:

Row 14: K to last st, M1L, k1. (44 sts)

Row 15: P1, M1L, p to end. (45 sts)

Rows 16–19: Rep rows 14–15 twice. (49 sts)

Row 20: Knit.

Row 21: P1, M1L, p to end. (50 sts)

Rows 22–25: Rep rows 20–21 twice. (52 sts)

Rows 26–28: Starting with a k row, work 3 rows st st.

Row 29: P1, M1L, p to end. (53 sts)

Rows 30–32: Starting with a k row, work 3 rows st st.

Row 33: P1, M1L, p to end. (54 sts)

Rows 34–53: Starting with a k row, work 20 rows st st.

Row 54: K1, skpo, k to end. (53 sts)

Row 55: Purl.

Rows 56–57: Rep rows 54–55 once. (52 sts)

Row 58: K1, skpo, k to end. (51 sts)

Row 59: P to last 3 sts, p2togtbl, p1. (50 sts)

Row 60: K1, skpo, pass the k st over the dec st, k to end. (48 sts)

Row 61: Purl.

Shape first ear

Row 62: Cast off 11 sts, k10, put the last 11 sts onto a stitch holder, cast off 15 sts, k10. Cut B and cont in A.

Work on this set of 11 sts only for the first ear.

Size

Completed creature measures approx. 19cm tall

Yarn suggestion

Lightweight yarn (such as Rowan Pure Wool DK) 2 x 50g balls in A (pink – Tea Rose 025) and 1 ball in C (dark pink – Hyacinth 026)

Super-fine-weight yarn (such as Rowan Kidsilk Haze) 1 x 25g ball in B (dark pink – Candy Girl 606)

Needles

Pair of 3.75mm knitting needles

Extras

One stitch holder

Tapestry needle

Washable toy filling

Oddments of black, pale green and white tapestry wool for embroidery

Tension

24 stitches and 36 rows to 10cm over st st using A and 3.75mm needles

Abbreviations

See page 126

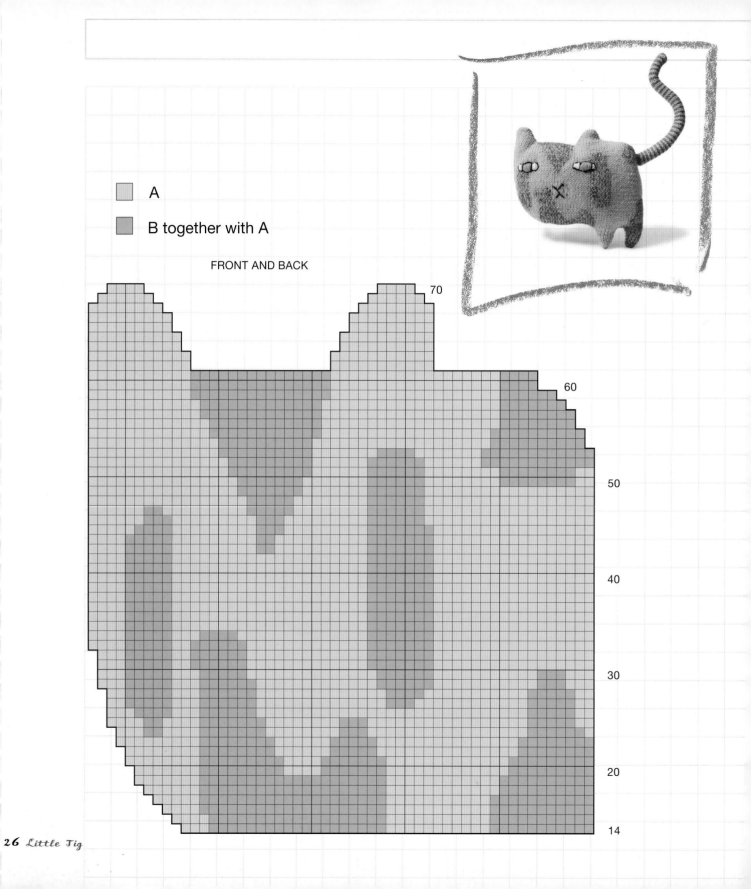

A

B together with A

FRONT AND BACK

70

60

50

40

30

20

14

Row 63: Purl.
Row 64: K1, skpo, k8. (10 sts)
Row 65: Purl.
Row 66: K1, skpo, k7. (9 sts)
Row 67: Purl.
Row 68: K1, skpo, k6. (8 sts)
Row 69: P1, p2tog, p2, p2togtbl, p1. (6 sts)
Row 70: K1, skpo, k2tog, k1. (4 sts)
Cast off.

Shape second ear
Put 11 sts on stitch holder onto a needle
and with WS facing, rejoin A.
Row 63: Purl.
Row 64: K to last 3 sts, k2tog, k1. (10 sts)
Row 65: Purl.
Row 66: K to last 3 sts, k2tog, k1. (9 sts)
Row 67: Purl.
Row 68: K to last 3 sts, k2tog, k1. (8 sts)
Row 69: P1, p2tog, p2, p2togtbl, p1. (6 sts)
Row 70: K1, skpo, k2tog, k1. (4 sts)
Cast off.

BACK
Work as given for Front,
reversing RS of work (to make
a mirrored pair of pieces) by reading knit
for purl and vice versa. See page 118 for
reverse shaping tips.

TAIL
Using the thumb method and C, cast on
67 sts.
Row 1: K2C, [k1A, k1C] rep to last 3 sts,
k1A, k2C.
Row 2: P2C, [p1A, p1C] rep to last 3 sts,
p1A, p2C.
Rep rows 1–2 seven more times.
Using C, cast off.

TO MAKE UP
Press pieces gently following directions on
the ball band.
Using mattress stitch, sew the body pieces
together around the outer edges, weaving
loose ends into seam wherever possible and
leaving a small opening. Insert toy filling and
sew opening closed.
Using mattress stitch and C, sew the two
long edges of the tail together by sewing
into the row two rows from the cast-on and
two rows from the cast-off edges and
around and through the stitches worked in C
only. This fills the tail as you seam it. If the
creature is not going to be given to a child,
you can push a length of wire into the tail to
allow you to shape it. Sew tail in position
with seam facing downwards.

Embroider as follows:
The face: for each eye, using black tapestry
wool and backstitch, embroider an oval with
a vertical line either side of the iris area. Fill
in the irises with satin stitch in pale green
and the areas on either side with satin stitch
in white; for the nose and mouth, using
black and backstitch, embroider an inverted
triangle with a vertical line descending from
the apex to touch the top of a second
triangle; for the whiskers, using black
embroider small straight stitches on both
cheeks. See also page 124.

Olive Owl may be small but she has a loud voice! People can hear her twit-twoos from ten miles away. Olive is very homely and likes housework and gardening. She makes a mean apple pie.

Olive Owl

pattern

FRONT
Using the thumb method and A, cast on 19 sts.

Join in B.
Starting with a knit (RS) row, strand the yarn not in use loosely across WS of work and work colour patt from the chart. Work shaping as follows:

Row 1 (RS): Knit.
Row 2: Purl.
Rows 3–16: Starting with a k row, work 14 rows st st.
Row 17: K1, skpo, k13, k2tog, k1. (17 sts)
Rows 18–30: Starting with a p row, work 13 rows st st.
Cut B and cont to work using A.

Shape first ear
Row 31: K4, put these 4 sts onto a stitch holder, cast off 9 sts, k3.
Work on this set of 4 sts only for the first ear
Row 32: P1, p2togtbl, p1. (3 sts)
Row 33: Knit.
Row 34: P1, p2togtbl. (2 sts)
Row 35: Knit.
Row 36: P2togtbl. (1 st)
Fasten off.

Shape second ear
Put 4 sts from stitch holder onto needle and with the WS facing, rejoin A.
Row 32: P1, p2tog, p1. (3 sts)
Row 33: Knit.
Row 34: P1, p2tog. (2 sts)
Row 35: Knit.

Row 36: P2tog. (1 st)
Fasten off.

BACK
Work as given for Front using A only.

BASE
Using the thumb method and A, cast on 11 sts.
Row 1: Knit.
Row 2: P1, M1L, p9, M1R, p1, (13 sts)
Row 3: K1, M1R, k11, M1L, k1, (15 sts)
Row 4: P1, M1L, p13, M1R, p1, (17 sts)
Starting with a k row, work 2 rows st st.
Row 7: K1, skpo, k11, k2tog, k1, (15 sts)
Row 8: P1, p2tog, p9, p2togtbl, p1, (13 sts)
Row 9: K1, skpo, k7, k2tog, k1, (11 sts)
Cast off.

WING PIECE ONE (make two)
Using the thumb method and A, cast on 5 sts.
Row 1: Knit.
Row 2: P1, M1L, p3, M1R, p1, (7 sts)
Row 3: K1, M1R, k3, M1L, k1, (9 sts)
Row 4: P8, M1R, p1, (10 sts)
Row 5: K1, M1R, k9, (11 sts)
Row 6: P10, M1R, p1, (12 sts)
Row 7: K1, M1R, k11, (13 sts)
Row 8: P10, p2togtbl, p1, (12 sts)
Row 9: Cast off 3 sts, k5, k2tog, k1, (8 sts)
Cast off.

Size
Completed creature measures approx. 14cm tall

Yarn suggestion
Lightweight yarn (such as Rowan Pure Wool DK) 1 x 50g ball in A (pink – Sugar Pink 038) and 1 ball in B (orange – Quarry 035)

Needles
Pair of 4mm knitting needles

Extras
One stitch holder
Tapestry needle
Washable toy filling
Oddments of black and grey tapestry wool for embroidery

Tension
22 stitches and 30 rows to 10cm over st st using 4mm needles

Abbreviations
See page 126

WING PIECE TWO (make two)

Using the thumb method and A, cast on
5 sts.

Row 1: Purl.
Row 2: K1, M1R, k3, M1L, k1, (7 sts)
Row 3: P1, M1L, p3, M1R, p1, (9 sts)
Row 4: K8, M1L, K1, (10 sts)
Row 5: P1, M1L, p9, (11 sts)
Row 6: K10, M1L, k1, (12 sts)
Row 7: P1, M1L, p11, (13 sts)
Row 8: K10, k2tog, k1, (12 sts)
Row 9: Cast off 3 sts, p5, p2togtbl, p1,
(8 sts)
Cast off.

TO MAKE UP

Press pieces gently following directions on
the ball band.

Using mattress stitch sew the body pieces
together around the outer edges, leaving the
cast-on edges open. Sew the base to the
cast-on edges, weaving the loose ends into
the seam wherever possible and leaving a
small opening. Insert toy filling and sew
opening closed.

Using mattress stitch, sew one of each wing
piece together around the outer edge,
weaving the loose ends into the seam
wherever possible and leaving a small
opening. Insert toy filling and sew opening
closed. Position the wings on either side
of the body so that the cast-off edge is
facing forward: this means for the left-hand
wing, wing piece two will be uppermost and
for the right-hand wing, wing piece one will
be uppermost.

Embroider as follows:

The face: for each eye, using black tapestry
wool and satin stitch, embroider a circle
with radiating straight stitches; for the
beak, using grey and satin stitch, embroider
a triangle.

The feet: for each foot, using grey tapestry
wool, embroider separate straight stitches
over the bottom of the front body onto the
base. See also page 124.

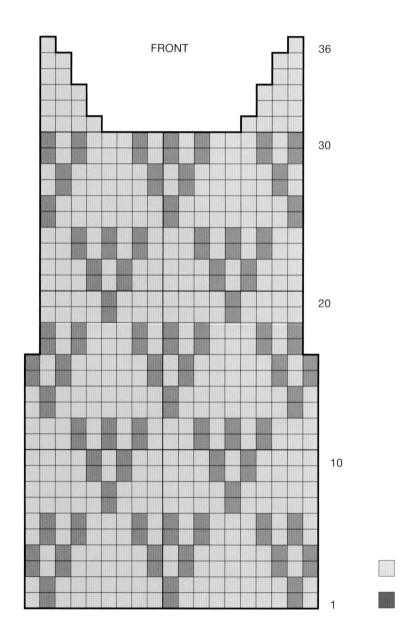

FRONT

36
30
20
10
1

▨ A
▨ B

Terry and Tina Twin are good friends, but I guess they'd have to be. Terry is calm and easy-going; Tina is small but feisty and usually gets her way. Terry likes reading and writing stories; Tina likes robots and dislikes bad breath.

Terry and Tina Twin

Size

Completed creature measures approx. 29cm tall

Yarn suggestion

Lightweight yarn (such as Rowan Cotton Glacé) 1 x 50g ball in A (light blue – Pier 809), 1 ball in B (deep mauve – Heather 828) and 1 ball in C (pink – Bubbles 724)

Needles

Pair of 3.50mm knitting needles
Set of four double-pointed 3mm knitting needles

Extras

One stitch holder

Waste cotton yarn

Tapestry needle

Washable toy filling

Oddments of black, green and white tapestry wool for embroidery

Tension

28 stitches and 44 rows to 10cm over st st using 3.50mm needles

Abbreviations

See page 126

pattern

FRONT BODY

First leg

Using 3.50mm needles, the thumb method and A, cast on 5 sts.
*Row 1 (WS): Purl.
Row 2: K1, M1R, k3, M1L, k1. (7 sts)
Row 3: Purl.
Row 4: K1, M1R, k5, M1L, k1. (9 sts)
Row 5: Purl.
Row 6: Knit.
Row 7: Purl.*
Row 8: K1, M1R, k to end. (10 sts)
Row 9: Purl.
Rep rows 8–9 twice more. (12 sts)
Cut yarn and put sts onto a stitch holder.

Second leg

Work as for First Leg from * to *.
Row 8: K to last st, M1L, k1. (10 sts)
Row 9: Purl.
Rep rows 8–9 twice. (12 sts)
Cut yarn and leave sts on the needle.

Join legs

Join in B.
Row 14 (RS): Knit across 12 sts on needle, cast on 22 sts using the backward loop method, with RS facing knit across 12 sts from stitch holder. (46 sts)

Body

Row 15: P11, p2tog, p20, p2togtbl, p11. (44 sts)
Starting with a k row, work 4 rows st st. Join in C.
Rows 20–25: Work in st st, using C and stranding B up the right-hand edge. (6 rows)
Rows 26–31: Work in st st, using B and stranding C up the right-hand edge. (6 rows)
Rep rows 20–31 three more times, then rep rows 20–25 once more.
Cut C and cont in B.
Starting with a k row, work 2 rows st st.
Row 76: K1, skpo, k to last 3 sts, k2tog, k1. (42 sts)
Row 77: Purl.

Row 78: As row 76. (40 sts)**
Row 79: P24, cast off 4 sts, p11. (24 sts on one needle. 12 sts on other)
Cut B 10cm from last st on needle and put sts onto a double-pointed needle.

BACK BODY

Work as for Front Body to **.
Row 79: P12, cast off 4 sts, p24. (12 sts on one needle, 24 sts on other)
Cut B 10cm from last st on needle and put sts onto a double-pointed needle.

ARMS

Arm fronts

***Using C, place a slip knot on a 3mm needle and with RS facing, pick up 6 sts along one edge of the last (uppermost) stripe of C on front body, cast on 1 st. Starting with a p row, work 7 rows st st.
Row 8: K1, skpo, k to last 3 sts, k2tog, k1. (5 sts)
Row 9: Purl.
Row 10: K1, skpo, k to last 3 sts, k2tog, k1. (3 sts)
Row 11: Purl.
Cast off.***
Rep from *** to *** on the other edge of the same stripe.

Arm backs

Work as for Arm Fronts, working on Back Body piece.

SMALLER HEAD

Leave the two sets of 12 sts from the body pieces on separate double-pointed needles, put rem sts onto waste yarn.
Split the sts from the Back Body onto two double-pointed needles. (6 sts on each needle)
Transfer 2 sts from each end of the group of sts from the Front Body onto the neighbouring needle holding sts from the Back Body piece. (8 sts on each of three needles)

With the Back Body piece facing, join in A on the left-hand needle and place round marker at this point.

Round 1: Knit.

Round 2: [K1, skpo, k2, k2tog, k1] three times. (6 sts on each needle) Knit 5 rounds.

Round 8: [K1, MIR, k to last st on double-pointed needle, MIL, k1] three times. (8 sts on each needle)

Round 9: Knit.

Rep rounds 8–9 three more times. (14 sts on each needle) Knit 12 rounds.

Round 28: [K1, skpo, k to last 3 sts on double-pointed needle, k2tog, k1] three times. (12 sts on each needle)

Round 29: Knit.

Rep rounds 28–29 once more. (10 sts on each needle) Rep round 28 twice more. (6 sts on each needle)

Round 34: [K1, skpo, k2tog, k1] three times. (4 sts on each needle)

Round 35: [Skpo, k2tog] three times. (2 sts on each needle)

Cut A 10cm from the last stitch on the needle and thread into a tapestry needle. Pass the tapestry needle through all the stitches on the needles in the order they would have been knitted, use the tip of the needle to pull the yarn at the point just after it has passed through the first stitch to draw the stitches tight to the yarn, then pull the yarn tight as it emerges through the last stitch. Secure the end.

LARGER HEAD

Place the two sets of 24 sts from the body pieces onto separate double-pointed needles.

Split the sts from the Back Body onto two double-pointed needles. (12 sts on each needle)

Transfer 4 sts from each end of the group of sts from the Front Body onto the neighbouring needle holding sts from the Back Body piece. (16 sts on each of three needles)

With the Back Body piece facing, join in A, on the left-hand needle and place round marker at this point.

Round 1: Knit.

Round 2: [K1, skpo, k10, k2tog, k1] three times. (14 sts on each needle) Knit 3 rounds.

Round 6: [K1, skpo, k8, k2tog, k1] three times. (12 sts on each needle) Knit 2 rounds.

Round 9: [K1, MIR, k to last st on double-pointed needle, MIL, k1] three times. (14 sts on each needle) Knit 3 rounds.

Rep rounds 9–12 once more. (16 sts on each needle)

Round 17: Knit.

Round 18: As round 9. (18 sts on each needle) Knit 24 rounds.

Round 43: [K1, skpo, k to last 3 sts on double-pointed needle, k2tog, k1] three times. (16 sts on each needle)

Round 44: Knit.

Rep rounds 43–44 once more. (14 sts on each needle)

Round 47: Knit.

Rep round 43 four more times. (6 sts on each needle)

Round 52: [K1, skpo, k2tog, k1] three times. (4 sts on each needle)

Round 53: [Skpo, k2tog] three times. (2 sts on each needle)

As for Smaller Head, cut A 10cm from the needle, thread into a tapestry needle and pass this through the rem sts, starting with the first st of the round, and draw tight.

TO MAKE UP

Press pieces gently following directions on the ball band.

Using mattress stitch, sew the body pieces together around the outer edge, weaving loose ends into seam wherever possible and leaving a small opening. Insert toy filling and sew opening closed.

Embroider as follows:

The faces: for each eye, using black tapestry wool and backstitch, embroider an oval with a vertical line either side of the iris area. Fill in the irises with satin stitch in green and the areas on either side with satin stitch in white; the mouth, using black and satin stitch, embroider a small mouth on each head. See also page 124.

Bunny Blue

Bunny Blue is fond of food, particularly picnics in the garden. If he can have his favourite raspberry cordial to drink, then he's very happy.

pattern

FRONT and BACK (both alike)

First leg

*Using the thumb method and A, cast on 5 sts.

Row 1 (WS): Purl.

Row 2: K1, M1R, k3, M1L, k1. (7 sts)

Row 3: Purl.

Row 4: K1, M1R, k5, M1L, k1. (9 sts)

Row 5: Purl.

Cut A and join in B.

Row 6: Knit.

Row 7: Purl.*

Row 8: K1, M1R, k to end. (10 sts)

Starting with a p row, work 3 rows st st.

Row 12: K1, M1R, k to end. (11 sts)

Row 13: Purl.

Cut yarn and put sts onto a stitch holder.

Second leg

Work as for First Leg from * to *.

Row 8: K to last st, M1L, k1. (10 sts)

Starting with a p row, work 3 rows st st.

Row 12: K to last st, M1L, k1. (11 sts)

Row 13: Purl.

Leave sts on needle and do not cut yarn.

Join legs

Row 14 (RS): Knit across 11 sts on needles, cast on 12 sts using the backward loop method, knit across 11 sts on stitch holder. (34 sts)

Shape body

Row 15: P10, p2tog, p10, p2togtbl, p10. (32 sts)

Starting with a k row, work 16 rows st st.

Shape arms

Row 32: K1, M1R, k to last st, M1L, k1. (34 sts)

Row 33: P1, M1L, p to last st, M1R, p1. (36 sts)

Rep rows 32–33 twice more. (44 sts)

Starting with a k row, work 4 rows st st.

Row 42: K1, skpo, k to last 3 sts, k2tog, k1. (42 sts)

Row 43: P1, p2tog, p to last 3 sts, p2togtbl, p1. (40 sts)

Rep rows 42–43 once more. (36 sts)

Starting with a k row, work 4 rows st st.

Shape first ear

Row 50: K9, turn.

**Work on this set of 9 sts only and put the rem stitches onto a stitch holder.

Starting with a p row, work 21 rows st st.

Row 72: K1, skpo, k3, k2tog, k1. (7 sts)

Row 73: Purl.

Cast off as follows: k1, skpo, pass the first st loop on the right-hand needle over the second, k1, pass the first st loop on the right-hand needle over the second, k2tog, pass the first st loop on the right-hand needle over the second, k1, pass the first st loop on the right-hand needle over the second.**

Shape second ear

Put next 9 sts on stitch holder onto needle, rejoin yarn with RS facing, k9, turn,

Rep from ** to **.

Shape third ear

Work as for Second Ear.

Shape fourth ear

Work as for Second Ear.

TO MAKE UP

Press pieces gently following directions on the ball band.

Using mattress stitch, sew body pieces together around the outer edges, leaving a small opening. Insert toy filling and sew opening closed.

Using C, make a small pom-pom and attach to back of the body.

Embroider as follows:

The face: for each eye, using black tapestry wool and backstitch, embroider an oval with a vertical line either side of the iris area. Fill in the irises with satin stitch in blue and the areas on either side with satin stitch in white; for the mouth, using pink, embroider a cross. See also page 124.

Size

Completed creature measures approx. 16cm tall

Yarn suggestion

Fine-weight yarn (such as Rowan Pure Wool 4 ply) small amount in A (light brown – Hessian 416), 1 x 50g ball in B (pale blue – Chalk 445) and small amount in C (cream – Snow 412)

Needles

Pair of 2.75mm knitting needles

Extras

One stitch holder

Tapestry needle

Washable toy filling

Oddments of black, blue, white and pink tapestry wool for embroidery

Tension

33 stitches and 44 rows to 10cm over st st using 2.75mm needles

Abbreviations

See page 126

Sleepy Pom is always dozing off — there's nothing he likes more than curling up in bed under his cosy duvet. He even dreams about sleeping!

Sleepy Pom

pattern

FRONT and BACK (both alike)

First leg

*Using the cable method and A, cast on 4 sts.

Row 1 (RS): Knit.
Row 2: Purl.
Row 3: Inc, k1, inc, k1. (6 sts)
Starting with a p row, work 3 rows st st.
Row 7: Inc, k3, inc, k1. (8 sts)
Starting with a p row, work 3 rows st st.
Cut A and join in B.
Cont in garter st (knit every row).
Knit 2 rows.*
Row 13: Inc, k to end. (9 sts)
Knit 5 rows.
Rep last 6 rows twice more. (11 sts)
Knit 2 rows.
Put sts onto stitch holder.

Second leg

Work as for First Leg from * to *.
Row 13: K to last 2 sts, inc, k1. (9 sts)
Knit 5 rows.
Rep last 6 rows twice more. (11 sts)
Knit 2 rows.

Join legs

Next row: Knit across 11 sts on needle, cast on 2 sts, knit across 11 sts on stitch holder. (24 sts)

Shape body

Knit 3 rows.
Next row: Skpo, k to last 2 sts, k2tog. (22 sts)
Knit 7 rows.
Rep last 8 rows twice more. (18 sts)
Knit 8 rows.

Shape arms

Next row: Cast on 7 sts, k to end. (25 sts)
Rep last row once more. (32 sts)
Knit 2 rows.
Next row: Skpo, k to last 2 sts, k2tog. (30 sts)
Knit 1 row.
Rep last 2 rows seven more times. (16 sts)

Shape head

Cut B and join in C.
Next row: Knit.
Next row: Purl.
Next row: Inc, k to last 2 sts, inc, k1. (18 sts)
Next row: Purl.
Rep last 2 rows seven more times. (32 sts)
Starting with a k row, work 4 rows st st.
Next row: Skpo, k to last 2 sts, k2tog.
Next row: P2tog, p to last 2 sts, p2togtbl.
Next row: Skpo, k to last 2 sts, k2tog.
Cast off.

TO MAKE UP

Do not press knitted pieces. Using mattress stitch, sew body pieces together around the outer edges, weaving loose ends into the seam wherever possible and leaving a small opening. Insert toy filling and sew opening closed.
Using A, make two pom-poms approx. 5cm in diameter. Sew one pom-pom to each top corner of head.
Embroider as follows:
The face: for each eye, using black tapestry wool and backstitch, embroider a half-circle; for the mouth, using red, embroider a cross. See also page 124.

Size
Completed creature measures approx. 30cm tall

Yarn suggestion
Medium-weight yarn (such as Lion Brand Vanna's Choice Baby) 1 x 100g ball in A (pale green – Sweet Pea 169), 1 ball in B (orange – Goldfish 132) and 1 ball in C (mint green – Mint 168)

Needles
Pair of 3.75mm knitting needles

Extras
One stitch holder
Tapestry needle
Washable toy filling
Oddments of black and red tapestry wool for embroidery

Tension
20 stitches and 30 rows to 10cm over st st using 3.75mm needles

Abbreviations
See page 126

TAIL UPPER

93
90

80

70

60

50

40

30

20

10

1

■ A

■ B

Cyril is from fox and squirrel descent. He's always been a keen storyteller and loves an audience to listen to his tales of adventure. He adores travelling and his great-great uncle was an infamous, sly red fox explorer. Cyril is totally in love with Rita Raccoon and they have two offspring — Ralf and Rill.

Cyril Squirrel~Fox

pattern

FRONT and BACK (both alike)

First leg

Using the thumb method and A, cast on 5 sts.

*Row 1 (WS): Purl.

Row 2: K1, M1R, k3, M1L, k1. (7 sts)

Row 3: Purl.

Row 4: Knit.

Row 5: Purl.

Rep rows 4–5 twice more.*

Row 10: K6, M1l, k1. (8 sts)

Row 11: Purl.

Cut yarn and put sts onto stitch holder.

Second leg

Work as for First Leg from * to *.

Row 10: K1 M1R, k6. (8 sts)

Row 11: Purl.

Leave sts on needle and do not cut yarn.

Join legs

Row 12 (RS): Knit across 8 sts on needle, cast on 10 sts using the backward loop method, with RS facing knit across 8 sts from stitch holder. (26 sts)

Body

Row 13: P7, p2tog, p8, p2togtbl, p7. (24 sts)

Starting with a k row, work 40 rows st st.

Shape arms

Row 54: K1, M1R, k to last st, M1L, k1. (26 sts)

Row 55: P1, M1L, p to last st, M1R, p1. (28 sts)

Row 56: K1, M1R, k to last st, M1L, k1. (30 sts)

Starting with a p row, work 4 rows st st.

Row 61: P1, p2tog, p to last 3 sts, p2togtbl, p1. (28 sts)

Row 62: K1, skpo, k to last 3 sts, k2tog, k1. (26 sts)

Row 63: P1, p2tog, p to last 3 sts, p2togtbl, p1. (24 sts)

Head

Starting with a k row, work 22 rows st st.

Shape first ear

Row 86: K12, turn.

Work on this set of 12 sts only and put the rem sts on stitch holder.

Row 87: P1, p2tog, p to end. (11 sts)

Row 88: K to last 3 sts, k2tog, k1. (10 sts)

Rep rows 87–88 three more times. (4 sts)

Row 95: Purl.

Cast off.

Shape second ear

Put sts on stitch holder onto a needle and with RS facing, rejoin yarn.

Row 86: Knit.

Row 87: P to last 3 sts, p2togtbl, p1. (11 sts)

Row 88: K1, skpo, k to end. (10 sts)

Size

Completed creature measures approx.
22cm tall

Yarn suggestion

Fine-weight yarn (such as Rowan
Pure Wool 4 ply) 1 x 50g ball in
A (orange – Spice 434) and 1 ball in
B (dark brown – Mocha 417)

Needles

Pair of 3mm knitting needles

Extras

One stitch holder

Tapestry needle

Washable toy filling

Oddments of dark brown, green and
white tapestry wool for embroidery

Tension

30 stitches and 40 rows to 10cm over
st st using 3mm needles

Abbreviations

See page 126

Rep rows 87–88 three more times. (4 sts)
Row 95: Purl.
Cast off.

TAIL UPPER

Using the thumb method and A, cast on
26 sts.
Join in B.
Starting with a knit (RS) row and stranding
yarn not in use loosely across WS of work,
work colour patt from the chart. Work
shaping as follows:
**Rows 1–30: Starting with a k row, work
30 rows st st.
Row 31: K1, M1R, k to last st, M1L, k1.
(28 sts)
Row 32: Purl.
Rows 33–34: Rep rows 31–32 once. (30 sts)
Rows 35–40: Starting with a k row, work
6 rows st st.
Row 41: K1, M1R, k to last st, M1L, k1. (32 sts)
Rows 42–54: Starting with a p row, work
13 rows st st.
Row 55: K1, M1R, k to last st, M1L, k1. (34 sts)
Row 56: Purl.
Rows 57–58: Rep rows 55–56 once. (36 sts)
Rows 59–64: Starting with a k row, work
6 rows st st.
Row 65: K1, M1R, k to last st, M1L, k1.
(38 sts)
Rows 66–86: Starting with a p row, work
21 rows st st.
Row 87: K1, skpo, k to last 3 sts, k2tog, k1.
(36 sts)
Row 88: Purl.
Rows 89–90: Rep rows 87–88 once. (34 sts)
Row 91: K1, skpo, k to last 3 sts, k2tog, k1.
(32 sts)
Row 92: P1, p2tog, p to last 3 sts, p2togtbl,
p1. (30 sts)
Row 93: K1, skpo, k to last 3 sts, k2tog, k1.
(28 sts) **
Cut B. Cont to work using A.
Row 94: [P1, p2tog] twice, [p2tog] eight
times, [p1, p2tog] twice, (16 sts)
Cast off.

TAIL UNDERSIDE

Using the thumb method and A, cast on
16 sts.
Using A only, work as for written instructions
for Tail Upper from ** to **, deducting 10 sts
from stitch totals given in brackets at the
end of the rows.
Cast off.

NOSE

Using the thumb method and A, cast on
28 sts.
Row 1 and every alt row (WS): Purl.
Row 2: K24, short-row-wrap the next
st, turn.
Row 4: K20, short-row-wrap the next
st, turn.
Row 6: K16, short-row-wrap the next
st, turn.
Row 8: K12, short-row-wrap the next
st, turn.
Row 10: K8, short-row-wrap the next
st, turn.
Row 12: K4, short-row-wrap the next
st, turn.
Row 14: K4, [pick up the short-row-wrap
and k tog with the wrapped st, k3] six times.
Rep rows 1–14, twice.
Cast off.

TO MAKE UP

Press pieces gently following directions on
the ball band.
Using mattress stitch, sew cast-on and
cast-off edges of nose together. Insert toy
filling into nose. Using mattress stitch, sew
nose to front of head, following photograph
for position.
Using mattress stitch, sew body pieces
together around the outer edges, weaving
loose ends into the seam wherever possible
and leaving a small gap. Insert toy filling and
sew opening closed.
Using mattress stitch, sew tail pieces
together around shaped outer edges,
weaving loose ends into the seam wherever
possible. Insert toy filling then sew cast-on
edges to back body, following photograph
for position.
Embroider as follows:
The face: for each eye, using dark brown
tapestry wool and backstitch, embroider an
oval with a vertical line either side of the iris
area. Fill in the irises with satin stitch in
green and the areas on either side with satin
stitch in white; for the nose, using dark
brown and satin stitch, embroider over the
tip of the knitted nose. See also page 124.

Oscar Dog

Oscar is a rare, stripy, sausage dog.
Because he has been blessed with
unusually good hearing, he can hear a
person coming up to ten miles away and
can sometimes hear what people are
saying in the next room.

Size

Completed creature measures approx. 38cm long

Yarn suggestion

Medium-weight yarn (such as Lion Brand Cotton-Ease) 1 x 100g ball in A (grey – Charcoal 152) and 1 ball in B (turquoise – Turquoise 148)

Needles

Set of five double-pointed 3.75mm knitting needles

Pair of 3.75mm knitting needles

Extras

One round marker

Tapestry needle

Washable toy filling

Oddments of black, blue and white tapestry wool for embroidery

Tension

21 stitches and 34 rows to 10cm over st st using 3.75mm needles

Abbreviations

MB = make bobble. Knit into front and back of next stitch six times, [turn, p6, turn, k6] three times, turn, p6, turn, [k2tog] three times, pass second then first stitch over third stitch

Note: use fifth double-pointed needle to work bobbles

See also page 126

pattern

STRIPE PATTERN

2 rows A.

2 rows B.

Work in stripe patt throughout stranding yarn not in use on WS.

BODY, HEAD and LEGS

Using 3.75mm double-pointed needles, the cable method and A, cast on 57 sts.
Arrange stitches over three needles, make sure stitches are not twisted and use fourth needle to knit first and last stitches together to join into the round. Place round marker at start of round.

Round 1 (RS): Knit. (56 sts)

Shape tail

Round 2: K26, s2tog, k1, psso, k27. (54 sts)

Round 3: K25, s2tog, k1, psso, k26. (52 sts)

Round 4: K20, skpo, k2, s2tog, k1, psso, k2, k2tog, k21. (48 sts)

Round 5: K22, s2tog, k1, psso, k23. (46 sts)

First back leg

Round 6: K19, skpo, s2tog, k1, psso, k2tog, k19, MB. (42 sts)

Round 7: K19, s2tog, k1, psso, k20. (40 sts)

Round 8: K16, skpo, s2tog, k1, psso, k2tog, k17. (36 sts)

Knit 5 rounds.

Second back leg

Round 14: K to last st, MB.

Body

Knit in rounds without shaping until work measures 25cm from cast-on edge, ending with an A stripe.

Shape head

Next round: Knit.

Next round: K18, M1, k18. (37 sts)

Knit 2 rounds.

Next round: K16, M1L, k5, M1R, k16. (39 sts)

Knit 2 rounds.

Next round: K14, M1L, k3, M1L, k5, M1R, k3, M1R, k14. (43 sts)

Knit 2 rounds.

Next round: K15, M1L, k4, M1L, k5, M1R, k4, M1R, k15. (47 sts)

First front leg

Next round: K to last st, MB.

Next round: K16, M1L, k5, M1L, k5, M1R, k5, M1R, k16. (51 sts)

Knit 5 rounds.

Next round: K21, skpo, k5, k2tog, k21. (49 sts)

Second front leg

Next round: K to last st, MB.

Next round: K20, skpo, k5, k2tog, k20. (47 sts)

Next round: Cast off 8 sts, k to last 8 sts, cast off. (31 sts)

Rejoin A to rem sts and work back and forth in rows using 3.75mm knitting needles.

Next row: K12, skpo, k3, k2tog, k12. (29 sts)

Next row: P1, p2tog, p to last 3 sts, p2togtbl, p1. (27 sts)

Shape nose

Work 4 rows st st.

Next row: K1, skpo, k8, skpo, k1, k2tog, k8, k2tog, k1. (23 sts)

Work 3 rows st st.

Next row: K1, skpo, k6, skpo, k1, k2tog, k6, k2tog, k1. (19 sts)

Next row: Purl.

Next row: K1, skpo, k4, skpo, k1, k2tog, k4, k2tog, k1. (15 sts)

Next row: Purl.

Next row: K1, skpo, k2, skpo, k1, k2tog, k2, k2tog, k1. (11 sts)

Next row: Purl.

Next row: K1, [skpo] twice, k1, [k2tog] twice, k1. (7 sts)

Cut yarn leaving a long tail. Pass yarn through rem 7 sts and pull up tight.

EARS (both together)

Using 3.75mm knitting needles, the thumb method and A, cast on 10 sts.

Cut A and complete ears in B.

*Row 1: Knit.

Row 2: Sl 1, k to end.

Rep row 2 twenty more times.

Row 23: K2tog, k to last 2 sts, k2tog.

Row 24: Knit.

Rep rows 23–24 once more, then rep row 23 once more.

Cast off.*

Carefully unpick A from cast-on edge and slip 10 sts onto needle.

Rep from * to *.

TO MAKE UP

Weave in all loose ends, weaving in ends on ears very neatly.

Turn body inside out then roll it back right side out over a rolled-up cotton tea towel, without stretching knitting out of shape, and steam. Leave to cool and remove tea towel. Pleat centre of ears and sew to top of head using backstitch and following photograph for position.

Using mattress stitch and matching the stripes, sew seam from tip of nose to base of chest. Insert toy filling from tail end. Using mattress stitch, sew up tail seam.

Embroider as follows:

The face: for each eye, using black tapestry wool and backstitch, embroider an oval with a vertical line either side of the iris area. Fill in the irises with satin stitch in blue and the areas on either side with satin stitch in white; for the nose using black and satin stitch, embroider over the tip of the knitted nose; for the whiskers, using white make fringe loops (as you would for the ends of a scarf) under stitches on each cheek. See also page 124.

Aggie is always doing washing — as soon as she has got one lot ready and dry, another load is ready to be washed. She does the washing for the whole neighbourhood. Sometimes she dreams of getting a new job.

Aggie Bear

pattern

HEAD, BODY, and LEGS

Head

Using 3.50mm double-pointed needles, the thumb method and A, cast on 49 sts. Arrange the stitches over four needles, make sure the stitches are not twisted and use the fifth needle to knit the first and last cast-on stitches together to join into the round. Place round marker at the start of the round. (12 sts on each needle)

Knit 2 rounds.

Thread a short length of waste yarn through a st loop at the end of the last round. This is the centre back.

Round 3: K10, M1R, k2 on first/third needle, k2, M1L, k10 on second/fourth needle. (13 sts on each needle)

Round 4: K11, M1R, k2 on first/third needle, k2, M1L, k11 on second/fourth needle. (14 sts on each needle)

Round 5: K12, M1R, k2 on first/third needle, k2, M1L, k12 on second/fourth needle. (15 sts on each needle)

Round 6: K13, M1R, k2 on first/third needle, k2, M1L, k13 on second/fourth needle. (16 sts on each needle)

Knit 1 round.

Round 8: K14, M1R, k2 on first/third needle, k2, M1L, k14 on second/fourth needle. (17 sts on each needle)

Knit 1 round.

Round 10: K15, M1R, k2 on first/third needle, k2, M1L, k15 on second/fourth needle. (18 sts on each needle)

Knit 10 rounds.

Round 21: K14, k2tog, k2 on first/third needle, k2, skpo, k14 on second/fourth needle. (17 sts on each needle)

Knit 24 rounds.

Round 46: K13, k2tog, k2 on first/third needle, k2, skpo, k13 on second/fourth needle. (16 sts on each needle)

Knit 12 rounds.

Round 59: K12, k2tog, k2 on first/third needle, k2, skpo, k12 on second/fourth needle. (15 sts on each needle)

Knit 3 rounds.

Round 63: K15 and move round marker to this point.

Sweater

Change to 4mm double-pointed needles and join in B.

Starting with a knit (RS) round, working in Fair Isle, stranding yarn not in use on the WS and weaving in yarn as required, work colour patt from chart. Read every chart round from right to left twice. Work shaping as follows:

Rounds 64–67: Knit 4 rounds.

Cut A and join in C.

Rounds 68–75: Knit 8 rounds.

Join in D.

Round 76: Knit using D.

Round 77: K1, M1R, k to end on first/third needle, k to last st, M1L, k1 on second/fourth needle. (16 sts on each needle)

Round 78: Knit.

Rounds 79–96: Rep rounds 77–78 nine more times. (25 sts on each needle)

Size

Completed creature measures approx. 50cm tall

Yarn suggestion

Lightweight yarn (such as Debbie Bliss Baby Cashmerino) 2 x 50g balls in A (pink – 340025)

Lightweight yarn (such Sublime Cashmerino Silk DK) 1 x 50g ball in B (black – Ebony 0013), 1 ball in C (red – Tease 0052) and 1 ball in D (maroon – Rhubarb 0107)

Needles

Set of five double-pointed 3.50mm knitting needles

Set of five double-pointed 4mm knitting needles

Extras

Round marker

Waste cotton yarn

Tapestry needle

Washable toy filling

Oddments of black and pink tapestry wool for embroidery

Tension

25 stitches and 36 rows to 10cm over st st using 3.50mm needles

Abbreviations

See page 126

Rounds 97–99: Knit 3 rounds.
Cut B, C and D and join in A.

Body

Change to 3.50mm double-pointed needles and rearrange the sts as follows:

Round 100: K40, put the next 20 sts onto a length of waste yarn, cast on 3 sts, k30, slip the next 20 sts onto a length of waste yarn (last 10 sts were knitted at the beg of this round) cast on 3 sts. (66 sts) (15 sts on first needle, 18 sts on second, 15 sts on third, 18 sts on fourth)
Knit 24 rounds.

First leg

Using only four of the five double-pointed needles, rearrange the sts as follows:

Round 125: K15, put the next 33 sts onto a length of waste yarn, k18, cast on 3 sts. (36 sts)
Arrange sts evenly over three double-pointed needles. (12 sts on each needle)
Knit 54 rounds.

*Round 180: [K1, k2tog] twelve times.
(24 sts in total)
Knit 2 rounds.

Round 183: [K2tog] twelve times.
(12 sts in total)
Knit 1 round.
Cut A 10cm from the last stitch on the needle and thread into a tapestry needle. Pass the tapestry needle through all the stitches on the needles in the order they would have been knitted, use the tip of the needle to pull the yarn at the point just after it has passed through the first stitch to draw the stitches tight to the yarn, then pull the yarn tight as it emerges through the last stitch. Secure the end.*

Second leg

With the First Leg to the right, transfer the first 12 sts from the length of waste yarn onto the first double-pointed needle, transfer the second 12 sts from the length of waste yarn onto the second double-pointed needle, transfer the last 9 sts onto the third needle and cast on 3 sts.

Knit 55 rounds.
Work as for First Leg from * to *.

First arm

Using only four of the five double-pointed needles, rearrange the sts as follows:
With the centre back to the right, transfer the first 8 sts from the length of waste yarn onto the first double-pointed needle, transfer the second 8 sts from the length of waste yarn onto the second double-pointed needle, transfer the last 4 sts onto the third needle and cast on 3 sts. (8 sts on first and second needles, 7 sts on third)
Knit 12 rounds.

Round 112: [K1, k2tog] seven times, k2.
(16 sts in total)
Knit 2 rounds.

Round 115: [K2tog] eight times, k1.
(8 sts in total)
Knit 1 round.
As for First Leg, cut A 10cm from the needle, thread a tapestry needle and pass this through the rem sts, starting with the first st of the round, and draw tight.

Second arm

With First Arm to the right, work as for First Arm.

EARS (make two)

Using 3.50mm double-pointed needles, the thumb method and A, cast on 16 sts.
Arrange the stitches over three needles, make sure the stitches are not twisted and use the fourth needle to knit the first and last cast-on stitches together to join into the round. Place round marker at the start of the round. (5 sts on each needle)
Knit 32 rounds.
Cast off.

TO MAKE UP

Press pieces gently following directions on the ball band.
Weave the loose ends into the WS of the body. Sew the head seam using mattress stitch. Insert toy filling and sew openings under both arms and between the legs closed using mattress stitch.
Bend the ears pieces around and sew to the head, following photograph for position.
Embroider as follows:
The face: for each eye, using black tapestry wool and backstitch, embroider a half-circle; for the mouth, using pink, embroider a cross. See also page 124.

SWEATER

99

90

80

70

64

A

B

C

D

Rill, Cyril's first child, is an enthusiastic camper and he loves catching grubs and worms to toast on the camp fire. He's full of energy and is always running around somewhere.

Rill Raccoon~Fox

pattern

Note: two strands of Rowan Scottish Tweed are used together throughout to even out the variable weight of the tweed yarn.

FRONT
First leg
*Using the thumb method and A, cast on 3 sts.
Row 1 (RS): Knit.
Row 2: P1, M1L, p1, M1R, p1. (5 sts)
Row 3: Knit.
Row 4: Purl.
Row 5: Knit.*
Row 6: P4, M1R, p1. (6 sts)
Cut yarn and put sts onto stitch holder.

Second leg
Work as for First Leg from * to *.
Row 6: P1, M1L, p4. (6 sts)
Leave sts on needle and do not cut yarn.

Join legs
Row 7: Knit across 6 sts on needle, cast on 10 sts using the backward loop method, with RS facing knit across 6 sts from stitch holder. (22 sts)

Body
Row 8: P5, p2tog, p8, p2togtbl, p5. (20 sts)
Starting with a k row, work 19 rows st st.

Shape arms
Row 28: P1, M1L, p18, M1R, p1. (22 sts)
Row 29: Cast on 3 sts using the backward loop method, k to end. (25 sts)

Row 30: Cast on 3 sts using the backward loop method, p to end. (28 sts)
Row 31: K1, M1R, k26, M1L, k1. (30 sts)
Starting with a p row, work 2 rows st st.
Row 34: P1, p2tog, p24, p2togtbl, p1. (28 sts)
Row 35: Cast off 3 sts, k to end. (25 sts)
Row 36: Cast off 3 sts, p to end. (22 sts)
Row 37: K1, skpo, k16, k2tog, k1. (20 sts)

Head
Join in B.
Using B and starting with a p row, work 6 rows st st.
Cut B and cont in A.
Row 44: Purl.

Shape first ear
Row 45: K8, k2tog, turn.
Work on this set of 9 sts only and put the rem sts on a stitch holder.
Starting with a p row, work 5 rows st st.
Row 51: K6, k2tog, k1. (8 sts)
Starting with a p row, work 11 rows st st.
Row 63: K1, skpo, k2, k2tog, k1. (6 sts)
Starting with a p row, work 3 rows st st.
Row 67: K1, skpo, k2tog, k1. (4 sts)
Row 68: Skpo, k2tog. (2 sts)
Cast off.

Shape second ear
Put sts on stitch holder onto a needle and with RS facing, rejoin yarn.
Row 45: K2tog, k8. (9 sts)

Size
Completed creature measures approx. 20cm tall

Yarn suggestion
Lightweight yarn (such as Rowan Scottish Tweed 4 ply used double) 2 x 25g balls in A (orange – Sunset 00011) and 1 ball in B (dark brown – Peat 00019)

Needles
Pair of 3.50mm knitting needles

Extras
One stitch holder
Tapestry needle
Washable toy filling
Oddments of white and dark brown tapestry wool for embroidery

Tension
18 stitches and 34 rows to 10cm over st st using yarn double and 3.50mm needles

Abbreviations
See page 126

Starting with a p row, work 5 rows st st.
Row 51: K1, k2tog, k6. (8 sts)
Starting with a p row, work 11 rows st st.
Row 63: K1, skpo, k2, k2tog, k1. (6 sts)
Starting with a p row, work 3 rows st st.
Row 67: K1, skpo, k2tog, k1. (4 sts)
Row 68: Skpo, k2tog. (2 sts)
Cast off.

BACK
Work as given for Front using A only.

TAIL
Using the thumb method and A, cast on
18 sts.
Row 1: Using A, knit.
Row 2: Using A, purl.
Join in B.
Row 3: Using B, knit.
Row 4: Using B, purl.
Last 4 rows form striped st st patt. Cont in
patt and work shaping as follows:
Work in 24 rows striped st st patt.
Row 29: Using A, [k3, inc] four times, k2.
(22 sts)
Work 15 rows in striped st st patt.
Row 45: Using A, [k4, inc, k4, inc] twice,
k2. (26 sts)
Work 21 rows in striped st st.
Row 67: Using B, [k4, k2tog, k4, k2tog]
twice, k2. (22 sts)
Row 68: Using B, purl.
Row 69: Using A, [k3, k2tog] four times, k2.
(18 sts)
Row 70: Using A, purl.
Cut yarn A.
Row 71: Using B, [k1, k2tog] six times.
(12 sts)
Row 72: [P2tog] six times. (6 sts)
Cut B 10cm from the last stitch on the
needle and thread into a tapestry needle.
Pass the tapestry needle through all the
stitches on the needles in the order they
would have been knitted, use the tip of the
needle to pull the yarn at the point just after
it has passed through the first stitch to

draw the stitches tight to the yarn, then pull
the yarn tight as it emerges through the last
stitch. Secure the end.

NOSE
Using the thumb method and A, cast on
12 sts.
Row 1 and every alt row (WS): Purl.
Row 2: K10, short-row-wrap the next st,
turn.
Row 4: K8, short-row-wrap the next st, turn.
Row 6: K6, short-row-wrap the next st, turn.
Row 8: K4, short-row-wrap the next st, turn.
Row 10: K2, short-row-wrap the next st,
turn.
Row 12: K2, [pick up the short-row-wrap
and k tog with the wrapped st, k1] five times.
Row 13: Purl.
Rep rows 2–13 once more.
Cast off.

TO MAKE UP
Press pieces gently following directions on
the ball band.
Using mattress stitch, sew cast-on and
cast-off edges of nose together. Insert toy
filling into nose. Using mattress stitch, sew
nose to front of head, following photograph
for position.
Using mattress stitch, sew the body pieces
together around the outer edges, weaving
loose ends into seam wherever possible and
leaving a small opening. Insert toy filling and
sew opening closed.
Using mattress stitch, sew tail pieces
together around the outer edge, leaving the
cast-on edges open. Weave in loose ends,
insert toy filling and sew cast-on edge to
back body piece, centred just above legs.
Embroider as follows:
The face: for each eye, working on the
brown band and using dark brown tapestry
wool and backstitch, embroider an oval with
a vertical line either side of the iris area. Fill
in the irises with satin stitch in dark brown
and the areas on either side with satin stitch
in white; for the nose, using dark brown and
satin stitch, embroider over the tip of the
knitted nose. See also page 124.

Stick the snail is a funny-looking fellow. He is very slow but a bit of a perfectionist — everything he does is done well. He even shines his shell twice a day. Stick has the nicest shell in town, everyone admires it, which makes all Stick's hard work worthwhile.

Stick Snail

Size

Completed creature measures approx.
21cm tall

Yarn suggestion

Lightweight yarn (such as Rowan Wool
Cotton) 1 x 50g ball in A (light brown –
Dream 929)

Lightweight yarn (such as Rowan Pure Wool
DK): 1 x 50g ball in B (pink – Petal 024)

Leftover lightweight yarns from your stash

Needles

Set of four double-pointed 3mm
knitting needles

Extras

Round marker

Waste cotton yarn

Tapestry needle

Washable toy filling

Oddments of black, white and pink tapestry
wool for embroidery

Tension

25 stitches and 36 rows to 10cm over st st
using 3mm needles

Abbreviations

See page 126

pattern

BODY and HEAD

Tail

Using the thumb method and A, cast on
37 sts.

Arrange the stitches over three needles,
make sure the stitches are not twisted and
use the fourth needle to knit the first and last
cast-on stitches together to join into the
round. Place round marker at the start of the
round. (12 sts on each needle)

Knit 63 rounds.

Now work back and forth on the three
needles in rows, not rounds.

Row 64: K34, short-row-wrap the next
st, turn.

Row 65: Sl1, p31, short-row-wrap the next
st, turn.

Row 66: Sl1, k29, short-row-wrap the next
st, turn.

Row 67: Sl1, p27, short-row-wrap the next
st, turn.

Row 68: Sl1, k25, short-row-wrap the next
st, turn.

Row 69: Sl1, p23, short-row-wrap the next
st, turn.

Row 70: Sl1, k21, short-row-wrap the next
st, turn.

Row 71: Sl1, p19, short-row-wrap the next
st, turn.

Row 72: Sl1, k17, short-row-wrap the next
st, turn.

Row 73: Sl1, p15, short-row-wrap the next
st, turn.

Row 74: Sl1, k13, short-row-wrap the next
st, turn.

Row 75: Sl1, p11, short-row-wrap the next
st, turn.

Row 76: Sl1, k9, short-row-wrap the next st,
turn.

Row 77: Sl1, p7, short-row-wrap the next
st, turn.

Row 78: Sl1, k5, short-row-wrap the next st,
turn.

Row 79: Sl1, p3, short-row-wrap the next
st, turn.

Row 80: Sl1, k3, pick up the short-row-wrap
and k tog with the wrapped st, short-row-
wrap the next st, turn.

Row 81: Sl1, p4, pick up the short-row-
wrap and p tog with the wrapped st, short-
row-wrap the next st, turn.

Row 82: Sl1, k5, [pick up the short-row-
wrap and k tog with the wrapped st] twice,
short-row-wrap the next st, turn.

Row 83: Sl1, p7, [pick up the short-row-
wrap and p tog with the wrapped st] twice,
short-row-wrap the next st, turn.

Row 84: Sl1, k9, [pick up the short-row-
wrap and k tog with the wrapped st] twice,
short-row-wrap the next st, turn.

Row 85: Sl1, p11, [pick up the short-row-
wrap and p tog with the wrapped st] twice,
short-row-wrap the next st, turn.

Row 86: Sl1, k13, [pick up the short-row-
wrap and k tog with the wrapped st] twice,
short-row-wrap the next st, turn.

Row 87: Sl1, p15, [pick up the short-row-
wrap and p tog with the wrapped st] twice,
short-row-wrap the next st, turn.

Row 88: Sl1, k17, [pick up the short-row-
wrap and k tog with the wrapped st] twice,
short-row-wrap the next st, turn.

Row 89: Sl1, p19, [pick up the short-row-
wrap and p tog with the wrapped st] twice,
short-row-wrap the next st, turn.

Row 90: Sl1, k21, [pick up the short-row-
wrap and k tog with the wrapped st] twice,
short-row-wrap the next st, turn.

Row 91: Sl1, p23, [pick up the short-row-
wrap and p tog with the wrapped st] twice,
short-row-wrap the next st, turn.

Row 92: Sl1, k25, [pick up the short-row-
wrap and k tog with the wrapped st] twice,
short-row-wrap the next st, turn.

Row 93: Sl1, p27, [pick up the short-row-
wrap and p tog with the wrapped st] twice,
short-row-wrap the next st, turn.

Row 94: Sl1, k29, [pick up the short-row-wrap and k tog with the wrapped st] twice, short-row-wrap the next st, turn.

Row 95: Sl1, p31, [pick up the short-row-wrap and p tog with the wrapped st] twice, p1, turn.

Row 96: Sl1, k34, pick up the short-row-wrap and k tog with the wrapped st.

Now work in rounds once more.

Round 97: Pick up the horizontal bar between the last and first sts of the round as if to M1R and k tog this bar with the first st, k to the end of the round.

Rounds 98–139: Knit 42 rounds.

First eye stalk

Round 140: K9, put 18 sts onto a length of waste yarn, cast on 1 st, k9. Rearrange stitches on the double-pointed needles so that there are 6 sts on the first and second needles and 7 sts on the third.

Knit 20 rounds.

Round 161: [K1, k2tog] six times, k1. (4 sts on the first and second needles, 5 sts on the third)

Round 162: Knit.

Round 163: [K2tog, k1] four times, k1. (9 sts in total)

Round 164: Knit.

Cut A 10cm from the last stitch on the needle and thread onto a tapestry needle. Pass the tapestry needle through all the stitches on the needles in the order they would have been knitted, use the tip of the needle to pull the yarn at the point just after it has passed through the first stitch to draw the stitches tight to the yarn, then pull the yarn tight as it emerges through the last stitch. Secure the end.

Second eye stalk

Transfer the next 18 sts from the waste onto two double-pointed needles, rejoin yarn with front facing,

Round 140: To starting working in the round, use a third needle to pick up 1 st from the base of First Eye Stalk, k6, use a fourth needle to k6, Use the needle that has now become free to k6, pick up 1 st from the base of the First Eye Stalk and cast on 1 st. (7 sts on the first needle, 6 sts on the second, 8 sts on the third)

Place round marker at the start of the round.

Round 141: K2tog, k5 on the first needle, k6 on the second needle, k5, k2tog, k1 on the third needle. (6 sts on the first and second needles, 7 sts on the third)

Rounds 142–160: Knit 19 rounds.

Round 161: [K1, k2tog] six times, k1. (4 sts on the first and second needles, 5 sts on the third)

Round 162: Knit.

Round 163: [K2tog, k1] four times, k1. (9 sts in total)

Round 164: Knit.

As for First Eye Stalk, cut A 10cm from the needle, thread a tapestry needle and pass this through the rem sts, starting with the first st of the round, and draw tight.

SHELL

Using the thumb method and B, cast on 37 sts.

Arrange the stitches over three needles, make sure the stitches are not twisted and use the fourth needle to knit the first and last cast-on stitches together to join into the round. Place round marker at the start of the round. (12 sts on each needle)

Rounds 1–2 (WS): Using B, knit.

Join leftover yarn. Leaving any ends to the outside (WS).

Round 3–4: Using leftover yarn, knit.

Rep the last 4 rounds, twisting the yarns at each colour change on the outside (WS), until the work measures 100cm.

Cast off.

TO MAKE UP

Press pieces gently following directions on the ball band.

Weave in the loose ends in the body, insert toy filling and sew opening closed using mattress stitch.

Weave in the loose ends in the shell, sew cast-on edge opening closed. Turn inside out, coil up the tube for about 30cm without any filling, then insert a little toy filling and gradually build up the amount of filling while continuing to roll the tube, sewing the coils together as it is rolled. Reduce the amount of toy filling toward the end and sew opening closed. Sew the shell to the body, following the photograph for position.

Embroider as follows:

The face: for each eye, using dark brown tapestry wool and backstitch, embroider an oval with a vertical line either side of the iris area. Fill in the irises with satin stitch in dark brown and the areas on either side with satin stitch in white; for the mouth, using pink and backstitch, embroider a double horizontal line. See also page 124.

Angry ginger is always grumpy, sometimes he is grumpy for no reason at all. Most of his friends know he is grumpy so they take no notice of him, which makes him even more grumpy! He has a soft spot for gingerbread — that can usually cheer him up.

Angry Ginger

pattern

Note: yarns A, B and C are worked held together throughout.

HEAD, BODY and LEGS

Using the thumb method and A, B and C held together, cast on 6 sts onto one needle.

Round 1 (WS): To start working in the round, slip half the stitches onto a second needle and position the two needles side by side with the first cast-on stitch and the last cast-on stitch adjacent on separate needles. Use a third needle to start knitting the round starting with the first cast-on stitch and working two stitches. Use a fourth needle to knit the next two stitches, one from each of the original two needles. (2 sts on each needle.) Complete knitting the round with the needle that has now become free. Place round marker at the start of the round.

Head

Round 2: [Inc] six times.
(4 sts on each needle)
Round 3: Knit.
Round 4: [K1, M1] twelve times.
(8 sts on each needle)
Rounds 5–6: Knit.
Round 7: [K3, inc] six times.
(10 sts on each needle)
Knit 20 rounds.
Round 28: [K4, inc] six times.
(12 sts on each needle)
Knit 2 rounds.

Shape arms

Round 31: K6, double-inc, k2, double-inc, k2 on the first needle, k12 on the second needle, k2, double-inc, k2, double-inc, k6 on the third needle. (16 sts on first needle, 12 sts on second, 16 sts on third)
Round 32: Knit.
Round 33: K16, turn work, p8 across the sts just worked, turn work and k8 on the first needle, k12 on the second needle, k8, turn work, p8 across the sts just worked, turn work and k16 on the third needle.
Round 34: K6, [skpo] twice, k2, [k2tog] twice on the first needle, k12 on the second needle, [skpo] twice, k2, [k2tog] twice, k6 on the third needle. (12 sts on each needle)

Body

Knit 16 rounds.

First leg

Round 51: [K14, cast off 3 sts] twice. Put the 15 sts not attached to the working yarn onto a length of waste yarn.
*Round 52: To start working in the round, k until 6 sts worked after cast off, use the free needle to k6, use the free needle to k3, cast on 3 sts using the backward loop method. (6 sts on each needle)
Knit 46 rounds.
Round 99: [K1, skpo, k1, k2tog] three times. (4 sts on each needle)
Knit 2 rounds.
Round 102: [Skpo, k2tog] three times. (2 sts on each needle)

Size

Completed creature measures approx. 36cm tall

Yarn suggestion

Medium-weight yarn (such as Rowan All Seasons Cotton) 1 x 50g ball in A (orange – Tangerine 230)

Super-fine-weight yarn (such as Rowan Kidsilk Haze) 1 x 25g ball in B (burgundy – Blood 627)

Super-fine-weight metallic yarn (such as Twilley's Washable Goldfingering) 1 x 1oz (25g) ball in C (gold – 02)

Needles

Set of four double-pointed 4mm knitting needles

Extras

Round marker

Waste yarn

Tapestry needle

Washable toy filling

Oddments of dark brown, green and white tapestry wool for embroidery

Tension

16 stitches and 28 rows to 10cm over st st using 4mm needles

Abbreviations

See page 126

Round 103: Knit.

Cut yarns 10cm from the last stitch on the needle and thread into a tapestry needle. Pass the tapestry needle through all the stitches on the needles in the order they would have been knitted, use the tip of the needle to pull the yarn at the point just after it has passed through the first stitch to draw the stitches tight to the yarn, then pull the yarn tight as it emerges through the last stitch. Secure the end.*

Second leg

Transfer the 15 sts from the waste yarn onto two double-pointed needles, rejoin yarn with First Leg to the right on the first st after what will become the gap between the legs.

Work as for First Leg from * to *.

TO MAKE UP

Press pieces gently following directions on the ball band.

Weave in the loose ends on the knit side (WS). Insert toy filling then sew opening between the legs closed using mattress stitch. Work a line of running stitch around each arm bump, draw tight and secure. Embroider as follows:

The face: for each eye, using dark brown tapestry wool and backstitch, embroider an oval with a vertical line either side of the iris area. Fill in the irises with satin stitch in green and the areas on either side with satin stitch in white; for the eyebrows, using dark brown and backstitch, embroider a slanting line above each eye; for the mouth, using dark brown and backstitch, embroider an oval opening and outline the teeth. Fill in the teeth with satin stitch in white.

The chest: using dark brown and straight stitches, embroider short, random lines. See also page 124.

Petra Poodle

Petra is a proud dog, she has excellent posture, is very conscious of her good looks and likes to be perfectly groomed at all times. She loves a good cup of tea after a long walk.

Size
Completed creature measures approx.
42cm tall, including head pom-pom

Yarn suggestion
Lightweight yarn (such as Debbie Bliss
Cashmerino DK) 2 x 50) balls in
A (cream – 18002)

Fine-weight yarn (such as Debbie Bliss
Rialto 4 ply) 1 x 50g ball in B (cream – 01)

Needles
Pair of 3.25mm knitting needles

Other materials
One stitch holder

Tapestry needle

Washable toy filling

15 x 10cm of thick wool felt or cardboard

Pins

Oddments of black, pale green and white
tapestry wool for embroidery

60 x 1cm of green craft felt

Tension
27 stitches and 36 rows to 10cm over
st st using 3.25mm needles

Abbreviations
See page 126

pattern

FRONT
Using A and the cable method, cast on
40 sts.

Starting with a k row, work 56 rows st st.

Shape back

Row 57 (RS): K33, put last 7 sts on
stitch holder.

Row 58: Purl. (33 sts)

Row 59: K to last 3 sts, k2tog, k1. (32 sts)

Row 60: P1, p2tog, p to end. (31 sts)

Rep rows 59–60 twice more. (27 sts)

Row 65: K to last 3 sts, k2tog, k1. (26 sts)

Row 66: Purl.

Rep rows 65–66 six more times. (20 sts)

Row 79: K to last 3 sts, k2tog, k1. (19 sts)

Row 80: Purl.

Row 81: Knit.

Row 82: Purl.

Rep rows 79–82 twice more. (17 sts)

*Neck

Starting with a k row, work 24 rows st st.

Shape head

Row 115: K1, M1R, k to last st, M1L, k1.
(19 sts)

Row 116: Purl.

Rep rows 115–116 six more times. (31 sts)

Starting with a k row, work 4 rows st st.

Row 133: K1, skpo, k to last 3 sts, k2tog,
k1. (29 sts)

Row 134: Purl.

Rep rows 133–134 once more. (27 sts)

Row 137: K1, skpo, k to last 3 sts, k2tog,
k1. (25 sts)

Row 138: P1, p2tog, p to last 3 sts,
p2togtbl, p1. (23 sts)

Rep rows 137–138 twice more. (15 sts)

Row 143: K1, [skpo] twice, k to last 5 sts,
[k2tog] twice, k1. (11 sts)

Row 144: P1, [p2tog] twice, p1, [p2togtbl]
twice, p1. (7 sts)

Cast off.*

Shape tail

Put 7 sts on stitch holder onto a needle and
with RS facing, rejoin yarn.

Starting with a k row, work 8 rows st st.

Next row: K1, skpo, k1, k2tog, k1. (5 sts)

Next row: Purl.

Cast off.

BACK
Using A, cast on 40 sts.

Starting with a k row, work 56 rows st st.

Shape back

Row 57 (RS): K7, put these 7 sts on stitch
holder, k to end.

Row 58: Purl. (33 sts)

Row 59: K1, skpo, k to end. (32 sts)

Row 60: P to last 3 sts, p2togtbl, p1. (31 sts)

Rep rows 59–60 twice more. (27 sts)

Row 65: K1, skpo, k to end. (26 sts)

Row 66: Purl.

Rep rows 65–66 six more times. (20 sts)

Row 79: K1, skpo, k to end. (19 sts)

Row 80: Purl.

Row 81: Knit.

Row 82: Purl.

Rep rows 79–82 twice more. (17 sts)

Work as for Front from * to *.

Shape tail

Put 7 sts on stitch holder onto a needle and
with WS facing, rejoin yarn.

Starting with a p row, work 7 rows st st.

Next row: K1, skpo, k1, k2tog, k1. (5 sts)

Next row: Purl.

Cast off.

BASE
Using A and the cable method, cast on
3 sts.

Row 1: Knit.

Row 2: Purl.

Row 3: K1, M1R, k to last st, M1L, k1.
(5 sts)

Row 4: Purl.

Rep rows 3–4 eight more times. (21 sts)

Starting with a k row, work 22 rows st st.

Row 43: K1, skpo, k to last 3 sts, k2tog, k1.
(19 sts)

Row 44: Purl.
Rep rows 43–44 seven more times. (5 sts)
Row 59: Skpo, k1, k2tog. (3 sts)
Row 60: Purl.
Cast off.

NOSE
Using A and the cable method, cast on
12 sts.
Row 1 (WS) and every alt row: Purl.
Row 2: K8, short-row-wrap the next st, turn.
Row 4: K4, short-row-wrap the next st, turn.
Row 6: K4, [pick up the short-row-wrap and
k tog with the wrapped st, k3] twice.
Row 7: Purl.
Rep rows 2–7 four more times.
Cast off.

EARS (make two)
Using A, cast on 9 sts.
Row 1: K1, p1, k5, p1, k1.
Row 2: K1, p7, k1.
Rep rows 1–2 fifteen more times.
Row 33: K1, p1, skpo, k1, k2tog, p1, k1.
(7 sts)
Row 34: K1, p5, k1.
Row 35: K1, p1, s2tog, k1, psso, p1, k1.
(5 sts)
Row 36: [K1, p1] twice, k1.
Rep row 36 twice more.
Cut yarn leaving a 20cm tail. Pass yarn
through rem 5 sts and pull up tight.

TO MAKE UP
Weave in loose ends on ears very neatly.
Press knitted pieces following instructions
on the ball band.
Using mattress stitch, sew cast-on and cast-
off edges of nose together. Insert toy filling
into nose. Using chain stitch or mattress
stitch as preferred, sew nose to front of
head, following photograph for position.
Using mattress stitch, sew body pieces
together around the outer edges from

cast-on edge, around body and head and
down to other end of cast-on edge, weaving
loose ends into the seam wherever possible.
Lay base on felt or cardboard and draw
around it. Cut out shape, cutting 5mm inside
drawn line. Lay felt or card shape on WS of
knitted base piece. Pin knitted base piece
into opening in bottom of the body and,
using mattress stitch, sew in place, leaving a
small opening. Insert toy filling and sew
opening closed.
Place ear against side of head, following
photograph for position, and place a pin in
the head at the top (cast-on edge) of ear.
Lay ear right side down across top of
head with cast-on edge against pin.
Using backstitch, sew across cast-on edge
to sew ear to head. Fold ear down over line
of sewing.
Using B, make three pom-poms approx.
3cm in diameter and one approx.
10cm in diameter. Sew one
small pom-pom to end of
each ear and to top of tail
and sew large pom-pom to
top of head.
Tie strip of craft felt in a bow
around neck.
Embroider as follows:
The face: for each eye, using
black tapestry wool and backstitch, embroider an oval with a
vertical line either side of the iris
area. Fill in the irises with satin
stitch in pale green and the areas
on either side with satin stitch in
white; for the nose, using black
and satin stitch, embroider over
the tip of the knitted nose. See
also page 124.

Vanessa is a fitness fanatic — she's been doing gymnastics since she was young — and fills her days with a strict regime of yoga, pilates and jogging.

Vanessa Hare

pattern

FRONT

Right leg

Using the cable method and A, cast on 8 sts.

Row 1 (RS): Knit.

Row 2: Purl.

Row 3: K2, M1R, k to last 2 sts, M1L, k2. (10 sts)

Row 4: Purl.

Rep rows 3–4 twice more. (14 sts)

Starting with a k row, work 15 rows st st.

Cut A and join in B.

Row 24: Purl.

Row 25: [K1, p1] twice, k2, M1R, k2, M1L, k2, [p1, k1] twice. (16 sts)

Row 26: P2, k1, p1, k1, p6, k1, p1, k1, p2.

Row 27: [K1, p1] twice, k8, [p1, k1] twice.

Rep rows 26–27 three more times, then rep row 26 once more.

Row 35: [K1, p1] twice, k1, C6F, [k1, p1] twice, k1.

Rep rows 26–35 six more times.

Row 96: P2, k1, p1, k1, p6, k1, p1, k1, p2.

Row 97: [K1, p1] twice, k8, [p1, k1] twice.

Rep rows 96–97 twice more, then rep row 96 once more.

Cut yarn and put sts onto stitch holder.

Left leg

Work as for Right Leg, but working C6B instead of C6F.

Leave sts on needle and do not cut yarn.

Join legs

Row 1 (RS): [K1, p1] twice, k8, [p1, k1] twice across sts on needle, cast on 4 sts, [k1, p1] twice, k8, [p1, k1] twice across sts on stitch holder. (36 sts)

Body

Row 2: P2, k1, p1, k1, p6, k1, p1, k1, p8, k1, p1, k1, p6, k1, p1, k1, p2.

Row 3: [K1, p1] twice, k1, C6B, k1, p1, k10, p1, k1, C6F, [k1, p1] twice, k1.

Row 4: P2, k1, p1, k1, p6, k1, p1, k1, p8, k1, p1, k1, p6, k1, p1, k1, p2.

Row 5: [K1, p1] twice, k8, p1, k10, p1, k8, [p1, k1] twice.

Rep rows 4–5 once more, then rep row 4 once more.

Row 9: [K1, p1] twice, k8, p1, k1, C4B, C4F, k1, p1, k8, [p1, k1] twice.

*Rows 10–11: As rows 4–5.

Row 12: As row 4.

Row 13: As row 3

Row 14: As row 4.

Row 15: As row 9.

Rows 16–19: As rows 4–5 twice.

Row 20: As row 4.

Row 21: As row 9.

Row 22: As row 4.

Row 23: As row 3

Rows 24–25: As rows 4–5.

Row 26: As row 4.

Row 27: As row 9*.

Rows 28–31: As rows 4–5 twice.

Row 32: As row 4.

Row 33: [K1, p1] twice, k1, C6B, k1, p1, k1, C4B, C4F, k1, p1, k1, C6F, [k1, p1] twice, k1.

Rows 34–37: As rows 4–5 twice.

Row 38: As row 4.

Row 39: As row 9.

Rep from * to *.

Size

Completed creature measures approx. 55cm tall, including ears

Yarn suggestion

Lightweight yarn (such as Rowan Wool Cotton) 1 x 50g ball in A (mauve – Billberry Fool 959) and 2 balls in B (lilac – Hiss 952)

Fine-weight yarn (such as Rowan Pure Wool 4 ply) small amount in C (cream – Snow 412)

Needles

Pair of 2.50mm knitting needles

Extras

Cable needle

One stitch holder

Tapestry needle

Washable toy filling

Oddments of black, blue, white and pink tapestry wool for embroidery

Tension

28 stitches and 49 rows to 10cm over moss st using 2.50mm needles

Abbreviations

See page 126

Rows 58–59: As rows 4–5.

Shape arms

Row 60: Cast on 6 sts, p2, [k1, p1] four times, k1, p6, k1, p1, k1, p8, k1, p1, k1, p6, k1, p1, k1, p2. (42 sts)

Row 61: Cast on 6 sts, [k1, p1] five times, k8, p1, k10, p1, k8, [p1, k1] five times. (48 sts)

Row 62: P2, [k1, p1] four times, k1, p6, k1, p1, k1, p8, k1, p1, k1, p6, [k1, p1] four times, k1, p2.

Row 63: [K1, p1] five times, k1, C6B, k1, p1, k1, C4B, C4F, k1, p1, k1, C6F, [k1, p1] five times, k1.

Row 64: As row 62.

Row 65: [K1, p1] five times, k8, p1, k10, p1, k8, [p1, k1] five times.

Rows 66–67: As rows 64–65.

Row 68: Cast off 6 sts, [p1, k1] twice, p6, k1, p1, k1, p8, k1, p1, k1, p6, [k1, p1] four times, k1, p2. (42 sts)

Row 69: Cast off 6 sts, p1, k1, p1, k8, p1, k1, C4B, C4F, k1, p1, k8, [k1, p1] twice. (36 sts)

Rows 70–71: As rows 4–5.

Row 72: As row 4.

Row 73: As row 3.

Row 74: As row 4.

Row 75: As row 9.

Rows 76–79: As rows 4–5 twice.

Row 80: As row 4.

Row 81: As row 9.

Row 82: As row 4.

Row 83: [K1, p1] twice, k1, slip next 3 sts onto cable needle and hold at back, knit next 3 sts on left-hand needle tog with 3 sts on cable needle, k1, p1, k10, p1, k1, slip next 3 sts onto cable needle and hold at front, knit next 3 sts on left-hand needle tog with 3 sts on cable needle, [k1, p1] twice, k1. (30 sts)

Collar

Row 84 (WS): Knit.

Knit 4 more rows.

Head

Starting with a k row, work 24 rows st st. Join in A.

Work 4 rows st st.

Change to B.

Row 117: Knit.

Shape first ear

Row 118: P8, put these 8 sts onto stitch holder, cast off until 7 sts rem on left-hand needle, p7.

Cont work on these 8 sts.

**Row 119: Knit.

Row 120: Purl.

Change to A.

Cont work in 4-row stripe patt until 7 more stripes completed.

Cast off.**

Shape second ear

Put sts on stitch holder onto a needle and with RS facing, rejoin yarn.

Work as for First Ear from ** to **.

BACK

Left leg

*Using the cable method and A, cast on 8 sts.

Row 1 (RS): Knit.

Row 2: Purl.

Row 3: K2, M1R, k2, M1L, k2, M1L, k2. (11 sts)

Row 4: Purl.

Row 5: K2, M1R, k to last 2 sts, M1L, k2. (13 sts)

Row 6: Purl.

Rep rows 5–6 once more. (15 sts)

Starting with a k row, work 15 rows st st.

Cut A and join in B.

Row 24: Purl.

Row 25: [K1, p1] to last st, k1.

Row 26: P2, [k1, p1] to last st, p1.

Rows 25–26 establish moss st with selvedge.

Cont as set until 79 rows of B worked.*

Cut yarn and put sts on stitch holder.

Right leg

Work as for Left Leg from * to *.

Leave sts on needle and do not cut yarn.

Join legs

Row 1 (RS): Moss across sts on needle,

cast on 3 sts, moss across sts on holder. (33 sts)

Body

Row 2: P2, [k1, p1] to last st, p1.

Row 3: [K1, p1] to last st, k1.

Rows 2–3 establish moss st with selvedge.

Cont as set until 59 rows of body worked.

Shape arms

Row 60: Cast on 6 sts, p2, [k1, p1] to last st, p1. (39 sts)

Row 61: Cast on 6 sts, [k1, p1] to last st, k1. (45 sts)

Work 6 rows in moss as set.

Row 68: Cast off 6 sts, [p1, k1] to last st, p1. (39 sts)

Row 69: Cast off 6 sts, [p1, k1] to last st. (33 sts)

Row 70: P2, [k1, p1] to last st, p1.

Row 71: [K1, p1] to last st, k1.

Cont in moss as set until 83 rows of body worked.

Collar

Row 84 (WS): K1, k2tog, k13, k2tog, k12, k2tog, k1. (30 sts).

Knit 4 rows.

Head

Starting with a k row, work 24 rows st st. Join in A.

Work 4 rows st st.

Change to B.

Row 117: Knit.

Shape first ear

Row 118: P8, put these 8 sts onto stitch holder, cast off until 7 sts rem on left-hand needle, p7.

Cont work on these 8 sts.

**Row 119: Knit.

Row 120: Purl.

Change to A.

Cont work in 4-row stripe patt until 7 more stripes completed.

Cast off.**

Shape second ear

Put sts on stitch holder onto a needle and with RS facing, rejoin yarn.

Work as for First Ear from ** to **.

TO MAKE UP

Do not press knitted pieces. Using mattress stitch, sew body pieces together around the outer edges, weaving loose ends into the seam wherever possible and leaving a small opening. Insert toy filling – but do not stuff the ears – and sew opening closed. You may find it easier to stuff the legs as you sew the seams. If the creature is not going to be given to a child, you can push lengths of wire into the legs and ears to allow you to shape them.

Using C, make a pom-pom approx. 5cm in diameter and sew to back above legs.

Embroider as follows:

The face: for each eye, using black tapestry wool and backstitch, embroider an oval with a vertical line either side of the iris area. Fill in the irises with satin stitch in blue and the areas on either side with satin stitch in white; for the mouth, using pink, embroider a cross. See also page 124.

Like cupcakes, doughnuts are a perfect treat — delicious and so low-fat! They also make excellent pincushions.

Iced Doughnut

pattern

DOUGHNUT

Icing

Using the thumb method and A, cast on 113 sts.

Arrange the stitches over four needles, make sure the stitches are not twisted and use the fifth needle to knit the first and last cast-on stitches together to join into the round.

Place round marker at the start of the round. (28 sts on each needle)

Knit 5 rounds.

Round 6: [K5, k2tog] sixteen times. (24 sts on each needle)

Knit 2 rounds.

Round 9: [K4, k2tog] sixteen times. (20 sts on each needle)

Knit 2 rounds.

Round 12: [K3, k2tog] sixteen times. (16 sts on each needle)

Knit 2 rounds.

Round 15: [K2, k2tog] sixteen times. (12 sts on each needle)

Knit 2 rounds.

Round 18: [K1, k2tog] sixteen times. (8 sts on each needle)

Knit 2 rounds.

Cut A and join in B.

Dough

Knit 8 rounds.

Round 29: [K2, M1R] sixteen times. (12 sts on each needle)

Knit 2 rounds.

Round 32: [K3, M1R] sixteen times. (16 sts on each needle)

Knit 2 rounds.

Round 35: [K4, M1R] sixteen times. (20 sts on each needle)

Knit 2 rounds.

Round 38: [K5, M1R] sixteen times. (24 sts on each needle)

Knit 2 rounds.

Round 41: [K6, M1R] sixteen times. (28 sts on each needle)

Knit 5 rounds.

Cast off.

TO MAKE UP

Press piece gently following directions on the ball band.

Using mattress stitch, sew piece together around the outer edge, weaving loose ends into the seam wherever possible and leaving a small opening. Insert toy filling and sew opening closed.

Embroider as follows:

The sprinkles: using pink, green, red and blue tapestry wool and individual straight stitches, embroider random short lines over half the icing surface.

Size

Completed doughnut measures approx. 12.5cm across

Yarn suggestion

Lightweight yarn (such as Rowan Cotton Glacé) 1 x 50g ball in A (white – Bleached 726)

Lightweight yarn (such as Rowan Wool Cotton) 1 x 50g ball in B (brown – Bronze 967)

Needles

Set of five double-pointed 3mm knitting needles

Extras

Round marker

Tapestry needle

Washable toy filling

Oddments of pink, green, red and blue tapestry wool for embroidery

Tension

25 stitches and 32 rows to 10cm over st st using 3mm needles

Abbreviations

See page 126

Ralf is the second of Rita and Cyril's offspring and by far the naughtiest. He once locked his brother, Rill, in a cupboard for over an hour!

Bad Ralf

pattern

FRONT

First leg

*Using 3.25mm needles, the thumb method and A, cast on 5 sts.

Row 1 (WS): Purl.

Row 2: K1, M1R, k3, M1L, k1. (7 sts)

Row 3: Purl.

Row 4: Knit.

Row 5: Purl.

Row 6: K1, M1R, k5, M1L, k1. (9 sts)

Row 7: Purl.*

Cut yarn and put sts onto a stitch holder.

Second leg

Work as for First Leg from * to *.

Leave sts on needle and do not cut yarn.

Join legs

Row 8: Knit across 9 sts on needle, cast on 10 sts using the backward loop method, with RS facing knit across 9 sts from stitch holder. (28 sts)

Body

Row 9: P8, p2tog, p8, p2togtbl, p8. (26 sts)

Starting with a k row, work 2 rows st st.

Row 12: K1, skpo, k20, k2tog, k1. (24 sts)

Starting with a p row, work 5 rows st st.

Row 18: K1, skpo, k18, k2tog, k1. (22 sts)

Starting with a p row, work 4 rows st st.

Shape arms

Row 23: P1, M1L, p20, M1R, p1. (24 sts)

Row 24: Cast on 3 sts using the backward loop method, k to end. (27 sts)

Row 25: Cast on 3 sts using the backward loop method, p to end. (30 sts)

Row 26: K1, M1R, k28, M1L, k1. (32 sts)

Starting with a p row, work 2 rows st st.

Row 29: P1, p2tog, p26, p2togtbl, p1. (30 sts)

Row 30: Cast off 3 sts, k to end. (27 sts)

Row 31: Cast off 3 sts, p to end. (24 sts)

Row 32: K1, skpo, k18, k2tog, k1. (22 sts)

Starting with a p row, work 3 rows st st.

Head

Join in B.

Using B and starting with a k row, work 4 rows in st st.

Cut B and cont in A.

Starting with a k row, work 2 rows st st.

Shape first ear

Row 42: K1, M1R, k10, turn.

Work on this set of 12 sts only and put the rem sts on a stitch holder.

Row 43: Purl.

Row 44: K1, M1R, k8, k2tog, k1. (12 sts)

Starting with a p row, work 3 rows st st.

Rep rows 44–47 once more.

Row 52: K1, M1R, k8, k2tog, k1. (12 sts)

Row 53: Purl.

Row 54: K1, skpo, k6, k2tog, k1. (10 sts)

Row 55: Purl.

Row 56: K1, skpo, k4, k2tog, k1. (8 sts)

Row 57: Purl.

Row 58: K1, skpo, k2, k2tog, k1. (6 sts)

Row 59: Purl.

Cast off.

Shape second ear

Put sts on stitch holder onto a needle and with RS facing, rejoin yarn.

Row 42: K10, M1L, k1. (12 sts)

Row 43: Purl.

Row 44: K1, skpo, k8, M1L, k1. (12 sts)

Size

Completed creature measures approx. 16cm tall

Yarn suggestion

Lightweight yarn (such as Rowan Wool Cotton) 1 x 50g ball in A (dark brown – Coffee Rich 956) and 1 ball in B (orange – Pumpkin 962)

Needles

Pair of 3.25mm knitting needles

Set of four double-pointed 3.25mm knitting needles

Extras

One stitch holder

Tapestry needle

Washable toy filling

Oddments of dark brown, blue and white tapestry wool for embroidery

Tension

23 stitches and 35 rows to 10cm over st st using 3.25mm needles

Abbreviations

See page 126

Starting with a p row, work 3 rows st st.
Rep rows 44–47 once more.
Row 52: K1, skpo, k8, M1L, k1. (12 sts)
Row 53: Purl.
Row 54: K1, skpo, k6, k2tog, k1. (10 sts)
Row 55: Purl.
Row 56: K1, skpo, k4, k2tog, k1. (8 sts)
Row 57: Purl.
Row 58: K1, skpo, k2, k2tog, k1. (6 sts)
Row 59: Purl.
Cast off.

BACK

Work as given for Front using A only.

TAIL

Using 3.25mm double-pointed needles, the thumb method and A, cast on 25 sts.
Arrange the stitches over three needles, make sure the stitches are not twisted and use the fourth needle to knit the first and last cast-on stitches together to join into the round. Place round marker at the start of the round. (8 sts on each needle)
Round 1: [K1, p1] rep to end of round.
Rep round 1 seven more times.
Round 9: [K1, M1R] rep to end of round. (48 sts)
Join in B.
Round 10: [K1A, k1B] rep to end of round.
Rep round 10 twenty nine more times.
Round 40: [K2togB, skpoA] rep to end of round. (24 sts)
Round 41: [K1B, k1A] rep to end of round.
Round 42: Rep round 41.
Round 43: [K2togA, skpoB] rep to end of round. (12 sts)
Round 44: [K1A, k1B] rep to end of round.
Round 45: [K2togB, skpoA] rep to end of round. (6 sts)
Cut A and B 10cm from the last stitch on the needle and thread A into a tapestry needle. Pass the tapestry needle through all the stitches on the needles in the order they would have been knitted, use the tip of the needle to pull the yarn at the point just after

it has passed through the first stitch to draw the stitches tight to the yarn, then pull the yarn tight as it emerges through the last stitch. Secure the end.

NOSE

Using 3.25mm needles, the thumb method and A, cast on 16 sts.
Row 1 and every alt row (WS): Purl.
Row 2: K14, short-row-wrap the next st, turn.
Row 4: K12, short-row-wrap the next st, turn.
Row 6: K10, short-row-wrap the next st, turn.
Row 8: K8, short-row-wrap the next st, turn.
Row 10: K6, short-row-wrap the next st, turn.
Row 12: K4, short-row-wrap the next st, turn.
Row 14: K2, short-row-wrap the next st, turn.
Row 16: K2, [pick up the short-row-wrap and knit tog with the wrapped st, k1] seven times.
Row 17: Purl.
Rep rows 2–17 once more.
Cast off.

TO MAKE UP

Press pieces gently following directions on the ball band.
Using mattress stitch, sew cast-on and cast-off edges of nose together. Insert toy filling into nose. Using mattress stitch, sew nose to front of head, following photograph for position.
Using mattress stitch, sew the body pieces together around the outer edges, weaving loose ends into seam wherever possible and leaving a small opening. Insert toy filling and sew opening closed.
Weave in loose ends on tail, insert toy filling and sew opening closed. Sew the tail to the back, centred just above the legs.
Embroider as follows:
The face: for each eye, working on the orange band and using dark brown tapestry wool and backstitch, embroider an oval with a vertical line either side of the iris area. Fill in the irises with satin stitch in blue and the areas on either side with satin stitch in white; for the nose, using dark brown and satin stitch, embroider over the tip of the knitted nose. See also page 124.

Mitten Kitten is very partial to midnight feasts. When everything is quiet she creeps downstairs and fixes herself a treat. So far no one has found out and Mitten would like to keep it that way!

Mitten Kitten

pattern

FRONT

Back leg

Using the thumb method and A, cast on 5 sts.

Row 1 (WS): Purl.
Row 2: K1, M1R, k3, M1L, k1. (7 sts)
Row 3: Purl.
Row 4: Knit.
Row 5: Purl.
Row 6: K1, M1R, k5, M1L, k1. (9 sts)
Starting with a p row, work 2 rows st st.
Row 9: P1, p2tog, p to end. (8 sts)
Cut yarn and put sts onto stitch holder.

Second leg

Using the thumb method and A, cast on 5 sts.

Row 1 (WS): Purl.
Row 2: K1, M1R, k3, M1L, k1. (7 sts)
Starting with a p row, work 3 rows st st.
Row 6: K1, M1R, k5, M1L, k1. (9 sts)
Starting with a p row, work 3 rows st st.
Cut yarn and put sts onto stitch holder.

Third and Fourth legs

Work as for Second Leg.
Leave sts of Fourth leg on needle and do not cut yarn

Join legs

Row 10: Knit across 9 sts on needle, [cast on 3 sts using the backward loop method, with RS facing, knit across 9 sts of the next leg] twice, cast on 3 sts using the backward loop method, k5, k2tog, knit across 8 sts of back leg. (43 sts)

Body

Row 11: P1, p2tog, p4, p2tog, p1, [p2togtbl, p7, p2tog] twice, p1, p2togtbl, p8. (36 sts)
Starting with a knit (RS) row, working in Fair Isle, stranding the yarn not in use on the WS and weaving in yarn as required, work colour patt from the chart. Work shaping as follows:
Rows 12–13:
Join in B.
Rows 14–15: Work in st st.

Row 16: K to last 3 sts, k2tog, k1. (35 sts)
Row 17: Purl.
Rows 18–19: Rep rows 16–17 once. (34 sts)
Row 20: K to last 3 sts, k2tog, k1. (33 sts)
Row 21: P1, p2tog, p to end. (32 sts)
Rows 22–23: Rep rows 20–21 once. (30 sts)
Row 24–31: Rep rows 16–17 four times. (26 sts)

Head

Join in C.

Rows 32–75: Starting with a k row, work 44 rows st st.

Shape first ear

Row 76: K10, put the last 10 sts onto a stitch holder, cast off 6 sts, k9.
Work on these 10 sts only for the first ear.
Row 77: P to last 3 sts, p2togtbl, p1. (9 sts)
Row 78: K1, skpo, k to end. (8 sts)
Rows 79–80: Rep rows 77–78 once. (6 sts)
Row 81: Purl.
Row 82: K1, skpo, k to end. (5 sts)
Rows 83–84: Rep rows 81–82 once. (4 sts)
Rows 85–87: Starting with a p row, work 3 rows st st.
Cast off.

Size

Completed creature measures approx. 24cm tall

Yarn suggestion

Lightweight yarn (such as Rowan Pure Wool DK) 1 x 50g ball in A (grey blue – Cypress 007), 1 ball in B (light blue – Pier 006) and 1 ball in C (dark blue – Navy 011)

Needles

Pair of 3.75mm knitting needles

Extras

One stitch holder
Tapestry needle
Washable toy filling
Oddments of black, green and pink tapestry wool for embroidery

Tension

24 stitches and 32 rows to 10cm over st st using 3.75mm needles

Abbreviations

See page 126

Shape second ear

Put sts on stitch holder onto a needle and with WS facing, rejoin B and C.

Row 77: P1, p2tog, p to end. (9 sts)

Row 78: K to last 3 sts, k2tog, k1. (8 sts)

Rows 79–80: Rep rows 77–78 once. (6 sts)

Row 81: Purl.

Row 82: K to last 3 sts, k2tog, k1.(5 sts)

Rows 83–84: Rep rows 81–82 once. (4 sts)

Rows 85–87: Starting with a p row, work 3 rows st st.

Cast off.

BACK

Work chart given for Back with written shaping as given for Front, reversing RS of work (to make a pair of pieces) by reading knit for purl and vice versa. See page 118 for reverse shaping tips.

TAIL

Using the thumb method and A, cast on 11 sts.

Starting with a knit (RS) row, working in Fair Isle, stranding the yarn not in use on the WS and weaving in yarn as required, work colour patt from the chart.

Rows 1–82: Work in st st.

Cast off.

TO MAKE UP

Press pieces gently following directions on the ball band.

Using mattress stitch and C, sew the long edges of the tail together 2 sts in from the edge, leaving the cast-on end open. This technique will fill the tail as you seam it. Following the photograph for position, pin tail to front body. Using mattress stitch, sew body pieces together around the outer edges, catching tail into seam, weaving loose ends into seam wherever possible and leaving a small opening. Insert toy filling and sew opening closed. If the creature is not going to be given to a child, you can push a length of wire into the tail to allow you to shape it.

Embroider as follows:

The face: for each eye, using black tapestry wool and backstitch, embroider an oval with a wide black line down the centre. Fill in the areas on either side with satin stitch in green for the nose and mouth, using pink and backstitch, embroider an inverted triangle with a vertical line descending from the apex. Embroider gently curving lines out to each side; for the whiskers, using black make fringe loops (as you would for the ends of a scarf) under stitches on each cheek. See also page 124.

FRONT   BACK

A

B

C

TAIL

82
80

70

60

50

40

30

20

10

1

Size
Completed creature measures approx.
9cm long

Yarn suggestion
Super-fine-weight yarn (such as Rowan
Kidsilk Haze) 1 x 25g ball in
A (dark brown – Villian 584) and 1 ball in
C (cream – Cream 634)

Embroidery thread (such as DMC embroidery
cotton) 1 x skein in B (yellow – 728)

Needles
Set of four double-pointed 2mm
knitting needles

Pair of 4mm knitting needles

Extras
Round marker

Tapestry needle

Washable toy filling

Oddments of black, blue, white and pink
tapestry wool for embroidery

Tension
30 stitches and 36 rows to 10cm over st st
using A and 2mm needles

20 stitches and 28 rows to 10cm over st st
using C and 4mm needles

Abbreviations
See page 126

Evel is a busy bee, most of the time he zooms around at 100 miles-an-hour looking for jobs to do. In his spare time he likes doing dangerous aerobatics: loop-the-loop is a favourite.

Evel Bee

pattern

HEAD and BODY

Using 2mm double-pointed needles, the thumb method and A, cast on 6 sts onto one needle.

Round 1 (RS): To start working in the round, slip half the stitches onto a second needle and position the two needles side by side with the first cast-on stitch and the last cast-on stitch adjacent on separate needles. Use a third needle to start knitting the round starting with the first cast-on stitch and working two stitches. Use a fourth needle to knit the next two stitches, one from each of the original two needles. (2 sts on each needle.) Complete knitting the round with the needle that has now become free. Place round marker at the start of the round.

Round 2 (RS): [Inc] six times.
(4 sts on each needle)
Knit 2 rounds.

Round 5: [Inc] twelve times.
(8 sts on each needle)
Knit 2 rounds.

Round 8: [K1, inc] twelve times.
(12 sts on each needle)
Knit 10 rounds.
Join in B.

Rounds 19–20: Using B, knit. (2 rounds)

Rounds 21–23: Using A, knit. (3 rounds)
Rep rounds 19–23 four more times.
Cut B.
Using A, knit 2 rounds.

Round 46: [K1, k2tog] twelve times.
(8 sts on each needle)
Knit 2 rounds.
Insert toy filling.

Round 49: [K2tog] twelve times.
(4 sts on each needle)
Knit 1 round.

Round 51: [K2tog] six times.
(2 sts on each needle)
Cut A 10cm from the last stitch on the needle and thread into a tapestry needle. Pass the tapestry needle through all the stitches on the knitting needles in the order in which they would have been knitted, use the tip of the needle to pull the yarn at the point just after it has passed through the first stitch to draw the stitches tight to the yarn, then pull the yarn tight as it emerges through the last stitch. Secure the end.

WINGS (both together)

Using 4mm needles, the thumb method and C, cast on 20 sts.

Row 1 (WS): Purl.
Row 2: Knit.
Row 3: P1, M1L, p to last st, M1R, p1.
(22 sts)
Row 4: K1, M1R, k to last st, M1L, k1.
(24 sts)
Row 5: P1, M1L, p to last st, M1R, p1.
(26 sts)
Rep rows 4–5 once more. (30 sts)

Row 8: Knit.
Row 9: Purl.
Row 10: Knit.
Row 11: P1, p2tog, p to last 3 sts, p2togtbl, p1. (28 sts)
Row 12: K1, skpo, k to last 3 sts, k2tog, k1. (26 sts)
Row 13: P1, p2tog, p to last 3 sts, p2togtbl, p1. (24 sts)
Rows 14–15: Rep rows 12–13. (20 sts)
Row 16: Knit.
Row 17: Purl.
Cast off.

TO MAKE UP

Lightly steam the pieces following directions on the ball band.

Pleat the centre of the wings and backstitch them to the top of the body, following photograph for position.

Embroider as follows:

The face: for each eye, using blue tapestry wool and satin stitch, embroider a stripe for the iris. On either side, embroider stripes with satin stitch in white; for the mouth, using pink and backstitch, embroider a gently curving line. See also page 124.

Bert is a friendly bear. He loves bubble-gum and can blow bubbles bigger than his head. He is known for his big appetite and keen sense of smell.

Bert Bear

pattern

FRONT and BACK (both alike)
First leg
*Cast on 8 sts.
Row 1 (RS): Knit.
Row 2: Purl.
Row 3: K2, M1R, k to last 2 sts, M1L, k2. (10 sts)
Row 4: Purl.
Rep rows 3–4 twice more. (14 sts)
Starting with a k row, work 12 rows st st.*
Cut yarn and put sts onto stitch holder.

Second leg
Work as for First Leg from * to *.
Leave sts on needle and do not cut yarn.

Join legs
Knit across 14 sts on needle, cast on 10 sts using the cable method, knit across 14 sts from stitch holder. (38 sts)

Shape body
Starting with a purl row, work 39 rows st st,

Shape arms
Next row: K2, M1R, k to last 2 sts, M1L, k2. (40 sts)
Next row: Purl.
Rep last 2 rows once more. (42 sts)
Next row: Cast on 8 sts, k to end. (50 sts)
Next row: Cast on 8 sts, p to end. (58 sts)
Next row: K2, M1R, k to last 2 sts, M1L, k2. (60 sts)
Next row: Purl.

Rep last 2 rows once more. (62 sts)
Next row: K2, skpo, k to last 4 sts, k2tog, k2. (60 sts)
Next row: Purl.
Rep last 2 rows once more. (58 sts)
Next row: Cast off 6 sts, k to end. (52 sts)
Next row: Cast off 6 sts, p to end. (46 sts)
Next row: Cast off 4 sts, k to end. (42 sts)
Next row: Cast off 4 sts, p to end. (38 sts)
Starting with a knit row, work 8 rows st st,

Shape head
Next row: K2, M1R, k to last 2 sts, M1L, k2. (40 sts)
Next row: Purl.
Rep last 2 rows twelve more times. (64 sts)
Starting with a knit row, work 6 rows st st.

Shape first ear
Next row: K28, put these 28 sts onto stitch holder, cast off 8 sts, k to end.
Cont work on these 28 sts.
Starting with a purl row, work 3 rows st st.
Next row: K2, skpo, k to end. (27 sts)
Next row: P to last 4 sts, p2togtbl, p2. (26 sts)
Rep last 2 rows once more. (24 sts)
**Starting with a knit row, work 6 rows st st.
Next row: K2, skpo, k to last 4 sts, k2tog, k2. (22 sts)
Starting with a purl row, work 3 rows st st.
Rep last 4 rows once more. (20 sts)

Size
Completed creature measures approx. 38cm tall

Yarn suggestion
Medium-weight yarn (such as Lion Brand Fishermen's Wool) 1 x 227g ball in brown – Nature's Brown 126
Note: *1 ball of Fishermen's Wool will make three bears.*

Needles
Pair of 3.25mm knitting needles

Extras
One stitch holder
Tapestry needle
Washable toy filling
Oddments of black, blue and white tapestry wool for embroidery

Tension
27 stitches and 35 rows to 10cm over st st using 3.25mm needles

Abbreviations
See page 126

Next row: K2, skpo, k to last 4 sts, k2tog, k2. (18 sts)

Next row: P2, p2tog, p to last 4 sts, p2togtbl, p2. (16 sts)

Rep last 2 rows twice more. (8 sts)

Next row: K2, skpo, k to last 4 sts, k2tog, k2. (6 sts)

Cast off purlwise.**

Shape second ear

Put sts on stitch holder onto needle and with WS facing, rejoin yarn to right-hand side of sts.

Starting with a purl row, work 3 rows st st.

Next row: K to last 4 sts, k2tog, k2. (27 sts)

Next row: P2, p2tog, p to end. (26 sts)

Rep last 2 rows once more. (24 sts)

Rep from ** to **.

NOSE

Cast on 4 sts.

Row 1 (RS): Purl.

Row 2: Inc, k to last 2 sts, inc, k1. (6 sts)

Row 3: Inc, p to last 2 sts, inc, p1. (8 sts)

Rep last 2 rows once more, then rep row 2 once more. (14 sts)

Row 7: Purl.

Row 8: As row 2. (16 sts)

Starting with a p row, work 5 rows st st.

Row 14: Skpo, k to last 2 sts, k2tog. (14 sts)

Row 15: Purl.

Row 16: As row 14. (12 sts)

Row 17: P2tog, p to last 2 sts, p2togtbl. (10 sts)

Row 18: As row 14. (8 sts)

Row 19: As row 17. (6 sts)

Row 20: As row 14. (4 sts)

Cast off.

TO MAKE UP

Block and press knitted pieces, pinning nose into a smooth circular shape and following instructions on the ball band.

Pin nose to centre of face, following photograph for position. Thread a tapestry needle with yarn and using chain stitch, sew around edge of nose to attach it to face. Before completing sewing, insert toy filling into nose.

Using mattress stitch, sew body pieces together around the outer edges, weaving loose ends into the seam wherever possible and leaving a small opening. Insert toy filling and sew opening closed.

Embroider as follows:

The face: for each eye, using black tapestry wool and backstitch, embroider an oval with a vertical line either side of the iris area. Fill in the irises with satin stitch in blue and the areas on either side with satin stitch in white; for the nose and mouth, using black and satin stitch, embroider an inverted triangle with a backstitch vertical line descending from the apex to touch the top of a backstitch circle. Outline one upper tooth in the circle with backstitch and black. See also page 124.

Fifi Flamingo

Fifi is a big gossip. She always wants to know what's going on and who has done what and she can chat for hours. Once she chatted on the phone to a friend in Australia for seven hours non-stop! The bill was enormous!

Size

Completed creature measures approx.
98cm from beak to tail

Yarn suggestion

Lightweight yarn (such as Debbie Bliss
Prima) 1 x 50g ball in A (black – 35701)

Lightweight yarn (such as Debbie Bliss
Baby Cashmerino) 1 x 50g ball in B
(bright pink – 3400129); 1 ball in C
(pink – 340016)

Needles

Set of four double-pointed 3mm
knitting needles

Extras

Round marker

Tapestry needle

Washable toy filling

Oddments of black, blue and white
tapestry wool for embroidery

Tension

25 stitches and 40 rows to 10cm over
st st using 3mm needles

Abbreviations

See page 126

HEAD and BODY

Beak

Using the thumb method and A, cast on
6 sts onto one needle.

Round 1 (RS): To start working in the round,
slip half the stitches onto a second needle
and position the two needles side by side
with the first cast-on stitch and the last
cast-on stitch adjacent on separate needles.
Use a third needle to start knitting the round
starting with the first cast-on stitch and
working two stitches. Use a fourth needle to
knit the next two stitches, one from each of
the original two needles. (2 sts on each
needle.) Complete knitting the round with
the needle that has now become free. Place
round marker at the start of the round.

Round 2: Knit.

Round 3: [Inc] six times.
(4 sts on each needle)
Knit 2 rounds.

Round 6: [Inc] twelve times.
(8 sts on each needle)
Knit 4 rounds.

Round 11: [K2, M1R] four times on first
needle, [K2, M1R] four times on second
needle, k8 on third needle. (12 sts on first
and second needles, 8 sts on third needle)
Knit 4 rounds.

Round 16: [K3, M1R] four times on first
needle, [K3, M1R] four times on second
needle, k8 on third needle. (16 sts on first
and second needles, 8 sts on third needle)
Knit 36 rounds
Cut A and join in B.

Round 53: Knit.

Round 54: [K1, p1] rep to end of round.
Rep round 54 ten more times.
Cut B and join in C.
Insert toy filling into beak.

Head

Round 65: Knit.
Purl 2 rounds.

Knit 30 rounds

Round 98: [K2, k2tog] ten times.
(12 sts on first and second needles, 6 sts
on third needle)
Insert toy filling into head.

Neck

Knit 194 rounds.
Insert toy filling into neck after approx.
every 30 rounds knitted.

Body

Round 293: [K3, M1R] ten times.
(16 sts on first and second needles, 8 sts
on third needle)
Knit 2 rounds.

Round 296: [K4, M1R] ten times.
(20 sts on first and second needles, 10 sts
on third needle)
Knit 2 rounds.

Round 299: [K5, M1R] ten times.
(24 sts on first and second needles, 12 sts
on third needle)
Knit 2 rounds.

Round 302: [K6, M1R] ten times.
(28 sts on first and second needles, 14 sts
on third needle)
Knit 2 rounds.

Round 305: [K7, M1R] ten times.
(32 sts on first and second needles, 16 sts
on third needle)
Knit 30 rounds.
Insert toy filling into body.

Round 336: [K6, k2tog] ten times.
(28 sts on first and second needles, 14 sts
on third needle)
Knit 2 rounds.

Round 339: [K5, k2tog] ten times.
(24 sts on first and second needles, 12 sts
on third needle)
Knit 4 rounds.

Round 344: [K4, k2tog] ten times.
(20 sts on first and second needles, 10 sts
on third needle)
Knit 8 rounds.

Round 353: [K3, k2tog] ten times.
(16 sts on first and second needles, 8 sts on third needle)
Knit 8 rounds.
Round 362: [K2, k2tog] ten times.
(12 sts on first and second needles, 6 sts on third needle)
Knit 8 rounds.
Insert toy filling.
Round 371: [K1, k2tog] ten times.
(8 sts on first and second needles, 4 sts on third needle)
Knit 8 rounds.
Insert toy filling into body.
Round 380: [K2tog] ten times.
(4 sts on first and second needles, 2 sts on third needle)
Knit 8 rounds.
Round 389: [K2tog] five times.
(2 sts on first and second needles, 1 st on third needle)
Round 390: Knit.
Cut C 10cm from the last stitch on the needle and thread into a tapestry needle. Pass the tapestry needle through all the stitches on the needles in the order they would have been knitted, use the tip of the needle to pull the yarn at the point just after it has passed through the first stitch to draw the stitches tight to the yarn, then pull the yarn tight as it emerges through the last stitch. Secure the end.

LEGS (make two)

Using the thumb method and B, cast on 12 sts onto one needle. Arrange sts over three needles so that there are 4 sts on each needle.
Place round marker at the start of the round.
Knit rounds until the work measures 62cm from the cast-on edge.
Next round: [K2tog] six times.
(2 sts on each needle)
Next round: Knit.
As for Body, cut B 10cm from the needle,

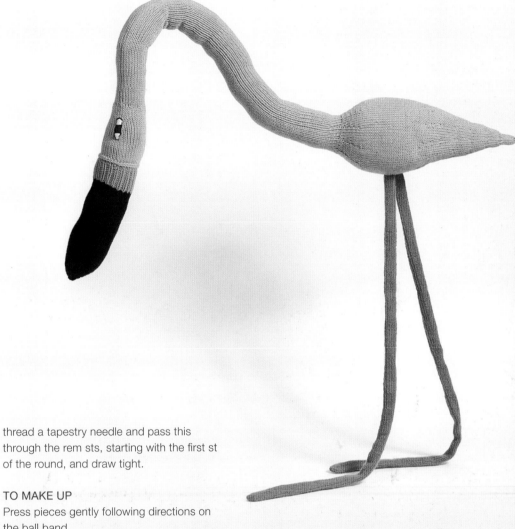

thread a tapestry needle and pass this through the rem sts, starting with the first st of the round, and draw tight.

TO MAKE UP

Press pieces gently following directions on the ball band.
Note that the legs are not stuffed.
Using mattress stitch, sew the legs to the underside of the body. If the creature is not being given to a child, you can insert a length of wire into the neck and bend it into shape.
Embroider as follows:
The face: for each eye, using black tapestry wool and backstitch, embroider an oval with a vertical line either side of the iris area. Fill in the irises with satin stitch in blue and the areas on either side with satin stitch in white. See also page 124.

Albert comes from a very small place so he doesn't like being around a lot of people and prefers country walks by himself. When he visits the city he has to wear earplugs as he thinks it's all too loud.

Lovely Albert

pattern

HEAD, BODY and LEGS

Head

Using 3.75mm double-pointed needles, the thumb method and A, cast on 57 sts. Arrange sts over four needles and use the fifth needle to knit the first and last cast-on sts together to join into the round. Place round marker at start. (14 sts on each needle) Knit 2 rounds.

Thread a length of waste yarn through st loop at end of last round. This is centre back.

Round 3: K13, M1R, k1 on first/third needle, k1, M1L, k13 on second/fourth needle. (15 sts on each needle)

Round 4: K13, M1R, k2 on first/third needle, k2, M1L, k13 on second/fourth needle. (16 sts on each needle)

Round 5: K13, M1R, k3 on first/third needle, k3, M1L, k13 on second/fourth needle. (17 sts on each needle)
Knit 1 round.

Round 7: K13, M1R, k4 on first/third needle, k4, M1L, k13 on second/fourth needle. (18 sts on each needle)
Knit 1 round.

Round 9: K13, M1R, k5 on first/third needle, k5, M1L, k13 on second/fourth needle. (19 sts on each needle)
Knit 1 round.

Round 11: K13, M1R, k6 on first/third needle, k6, M1L, k13 on second/fourth needle. (20 sts on each needle)
Knit 1 round.

Round 13: K13, M1R, k7 on first/third needle, k7, M1L, k13 on second/fourth needle. (21 sts on each needle)
Knit 2 rounds.

Round 16: K13, M1R, k8 on first/third needle, k8, M1L, k13 on second/fourth needle. (22 sts on each needle)
Knit 2 rounds.

Round 19: K13, M1R, k9 on first/third needle, k9, M1L, k13 on second/fourth needle. (23 sts on each needle)
Knit 2 rounds.

Round 22: K13, M1R, k10 on first/third needle, k10, M1L, k13 on second/fourth needle. (24 sts on each needle)

Separate stitches for ears

Round 23: K13, put the next 22 sts onto a length of waste yarn, cast on 4 sts, k26, slip the next 22 sts onto a length of waste yarn, cast on 4 sts, k13. (60 sts)
Arrange 15 stitches on each of four needles.

Body

Knit 7 rounds.

Round 31: K11, k2tog, k2 on first/third needle, k2, skpo, k11 on second/fourth needle. (14 sts on each needle)
Knit 7 rounds.

Size
Completed creature measures approx. 16cm tall

Yarn suggestion
Medium-weight yarn (such as Sublime Angora Merino) 1 x 50g ball in A (blue – Dusky 0047) and 1 ball in B (white – Feather 040)

Needles
Set of five double-pointed 3.75mm knitting needles
Pair of 3.75 knitting needles.

Extras
Round marker
Waste cotton yarn
Tapestry needle
Washable toy filling
Oddments of black, blue and white tapestry wool for embroidery
1.5 x 26cm of blue craft felt

Tension
25 stitches and 36 rows to 10cm over st st using 3.75mm needles

Abbreviations
See page 126

Round 39: K10, k2tog, k2 on first/third needle, k2, skpo, k10 on second/fourth needle. (13 sts on each needle)
Knit 7 rounds.
Round 47: K9, k2tog, k2 on first/third needle, k2, skpo, k9 on second/fourth needle. (12 sts on each needle)
Knit 2 rounds.
Round 50: K11, M1L, k1 on first/third needle, k1, M1R, k11 on second/fourth needle. (13 sts on each needle)
Knit 1 round.
Round 52: K12, M1L, k1 on first/third needle, k1, M1R, k12 on second/fourth needle. (14 sts on each needle)
Knit 1 round.

First leg

Using only four of the five double-pointed needles, rearrange the sts as follows:
Round 54: K21, put the next 21 sts onto a length of waste yarn, put the following 21 sts on a second length of waste yarn (the last 7 of these sts were knitted at the beg of the round), cast on 1 st.
Working clockwise, thread a short length of waste yarn through the st loop before the cast-on st and rep with a second length of waste yarn through the st after the cast-on st. The st after the cast-on st is the start of the round for First Leg only. (15 sts)
Arrange sts evenly over three double-pointed needles.
Knit 5 rounds.
Round 60: [K1, k2tog] five times. (10 sts in total)
Knit 1 round.
Cut A 10cm from last stitch on needle and thread into a tapestry needle. Pass tapestry needle through all the stitches on the needles in the order they would have been knitted, use the tip of the needle to pull the yarn at the point just after it has passed through the first stitch to draw the stitches tight to the yarn, then pull the yarn tight as it emerges through the last stitch. Secure end.

Second leg

With the First Leg to the right, transfer the first 7 sts from the first length of waste yarn and the last 7 sts from the second length of waste yarn onto two separate double-pointed needles.
Round 54: Using a third needle, pick up 1 st through first marked st of the First Leg, k5, using a fourth needle, k2, cast on 1 st, k2, using needle that has now become free k5, pick up 1 st through second marked st of the First Leg then pick up one st through the cast on stitch of the First Leg. (6 sts on first needle, 5 sts on second, 7 sts on third)
As for First Leg, thread short lengths of waste yarn through the st loops before the cast-on st and after the cast-on st created on this round.
Round 55: K2tog, k4 on first needle, k5 on second needle, k4, k2tog, k1 on third needle. (5 sts on first and second needles, 6 sts on third)
Knit 4 rounds.
Round 60: K2tog, [k2tog, k1] four times, k2tog. (10 sts in total)
Knit 1 round.
As for the First Leg, cut A 10cm from the needle, thread a tapestry needle and pass this through the rem sts, starting with the first st of the round, and draw tight.

Third leg

Work as for Second Leg.

Fourth leg

With the Third Leg to the right, transfer the first 7 sts from the first length of waste yarn and the last 7 sts from the second length of waste yarn onto two separate double-pointed needles.
Round 54: Using a third needle, pick up 1 st through the first marked st of the third leg, k5, using a fourth needle, k5, using the needle that has now become free k4, pick up 1 st through the second marked st of the third leg then pick up one st through the cast-on stitch of the third leg. (6 sts on first

needle, 5 sts on second, 6 sts on third)
Round 55: K2tog, k4 on first needle, k5 on second needle, k3, k2tog, k1 on third needle. (5 sts on each needle)
Knit 4 rounds.
Round 60: [K1, k2tog] five times. (10 sts in total)
Knit 1 round.
As for the First Leg, cut A 10cm from the needle, thread a tapestry needle and pass this through the rem sts, starting with the first st of the round, and draw tight.

First ear

With the centre back to the right, arrange the sts as follows onto four double-pointed needles: transfer 7 sts from the waste yarn onto the first needle, 7 sts onto the second needle, 7 sts onto the third needle and 1 st onto the fourth needle. Join A to the first st of the first needle.
Round 24: K7 on each of the first three needles, k1, pick up 1 st from the nearest body st, pick up 1 st in each of the 4 cast-on sts, pick up 1 st from the next body st for the fourth needle. (7 sts on each needle)
Knit 6 rounds.
Round 31: K7 on each of the first three needles, k1, k2tog, k1, skpo, k1 on the fourth needle. (7 sts on each of first three needles, 5 sts on fourth)
Knit 1 round.
Round 33: Skpo, k5 on first needle, k7 on second needle, k5, k2tog on third needle, k5 on fourth needle. (6 sts on first needle, 7 sts on second, 6 sts on third, 5 sts on fourth)
Knit 1 round.
Round 35: Skpo, k4 on first needle, k7 on second needle, k4, k2tog on third needle, k5 on fourth needle. (5 sts on first needle, 7 sts on second 5 sts on third and fourth)
Knit 1 round.
Round 37: Skpo, k3 on first needle, k7 on second needle, k3, k2tog on third needle, k5 on fourth needle. (4 sts on first needle, 7 sts on second, 4 sts on third, 5 sts on fourth)

Knit 1 round.

Round 39: Skpo, k2 on first needle, k7 on second needle, k2, k2tog on third needle, k5 on fourth needle. (3 sts on first needle, 7 sts on second, 3 sts on third, 5 sts on fourth)

Discard one needle and rearrange sts so that there are 6 sts on each needle.

Knit 21 rounds.

Round 61: [K1, k2tog] six times. (12 sts in total)

Knit 1 round.

Round 63: [K1, k2tog] four times. (8 sts in total)

Knit 1 round.

As for First Leg, cut A 10cm from the needle, thread a tapestry needle and pass this through the rem sts, starting with the first st of the round, and draw tight.

Second ear

With the First Ear to the right and the front facing, work as for First Ear.

NOSE

Using 3.75mm needles, the thumb method and B, cast on 7 sts.

Row 1 (WS): Purl.

Row 2: Knit.

Row 3: Purl.

Row 4: K1, M1R, k to last st, M1L, k1. (9 sts)

Rows 5–7: Work in st st.

Rep rows 4–7 three more times. (15 sts)

Row 20: K1, M1R, k to last st, M1L, k1. (17 sts)

Row 21: Purl.

Row 22: K1, M1R, k6, s2tog, k1, psso, k6, M1L, k1.

Row 23: Purl.

Row 24: K1, M1R, k7, sl1 k7, M1L, k1. (19 sts)

Row 25: Purl.

Row 26: K1, M1R, k7, s2tog, k1, psso, k7, M1L, k1.

Row 27: Purl.

Row 28: K1, M1R, k8, sl1 k8, M1L, k1. (21 sts)

Row 29: Purl.

Row 30: K9, s2tog, k1, psso, k9. (19 sts)

Row 31: Purl.

Row 32: K9, sl1, k9.

Row 33: Purl.

Row 34: K8, s2tog, k1, psso, k8. (17 sts)

Row 35: Purl.

Row 36: K7, s2tog, k1, psso, k7. (15 sts)

Row 37: Purl.

Cast off 5 sts, s2tog, k1, psso, pass the st furthest from the tip on the right-hand needle over the st nearest the tip, cont to cast off to the end of the row. Fasten off.

TO MAKE UP

Press pieces gently following directions on the ball band.

Weave the loose ends into the WS of the body, insert toy filling and sew opening closed using mattress stitch.

Following the photograph for position, pin the nose to the front. Using mattress stitch and leaving an opening, sew the nose to the body around the outer edge, insert toy filling and sew opening closed.

Embroider as follows:

The face: for each eye, using black tapestry wool and backstitch, embroider an oval with a vertical line either side of the iris area. Fill in the irises with satin stitch in blue and the areas on either side with satin stitch in white; for the nose, using black and satin stitch, embroider an inverted triangle. See also page 124.

Cut the felt to fit around Albert's neck and sew the ends of the collar together around his neck.

Humphrey would love to be a prince or even a king!
He adores relaxing and getting things done for him.
Sometimes he dresses up in front of the mirror with
a pretend crown he has made out of cardboard!

Humphrey Hare

pattern

Size
Completed creature measures approx. 37cm tall, including ears.

Yarn suggestion
Fine-weight yarn (such as Lion Brand Sock Ease) 1 x 100g ball in variegated grey/brown/yellow – Rock Candy 201
Fine-weight yarn (such as Rowan Pure Wool 4 ply) small amount in C (cream – Snow 412)

Needles
Pair of 2.25mm knitting needles

Extras
Tapestry needle
Washable toy filling
Oddments of black, blue, white and pink tapestry wool for embroidery

Tension
34 stitches and 48 rows to 10cm over st st using 2.25mm needles.

Abbreviations
See page 126

BODY, LEGS and EARS
Note: *this section is knitted sideways in one piece, starting at centre back.*
Using the cable method, cast on 60 sts.
Row 1 (RS): Knit.
Row 2: Purl.
Shape leg
*Row 3: Cast on 33 sts, k to end. (93 sts)
Row 4: Purl.
Row 5: Cast on 3 sts, k to end. (96 sts)
Row 6: Purl.
Rep rows 5–6 once more. (99 sts)
Starting with a k row, work 3 rows st st.
Shape ear
Row 12: Cast on 30 sts, p to end. (129 sts)
Starting with a k row, work 4 rows st st.
Row 17: Cast off 3 sts, k to end. (126 sts)
Row 18: Purl.
Rep rows 17–18 once more. (123 sts)
Row 21: Cast on 3 sts, k to end. (126 sts)
Row 22: Purl.
Rep rows 21–22 once more. (129 sts)
Starting with a k row, work 3 rows st st.
Row 28: Cast off 30 sts, p to end. (99 sts)
Starting with a k row, work 4 rows st st.
Row 33: Cast off 3 sts, k to end. (96 sts)
Row 34: Purl.
Rep rows 33–34 once more. (93 sts)
Row 37: Cast off 33 sts, k to end. (60 sts)*
Starting with a p row, work 3 rows st st.
Rep from * to *.
Starting with a p row, work 2 rows st st.
Cast off.

ARMS (make two)
Cast on 18 sts.
Starting with a k row, work 8 rows st st.
Cast off.

TO MAKE UP
Press knitted pieces following instructions on the ball band.
Using mattress stitch, sew first cast-on and last cast-off edges together for centre back seam. With seam at centre back, sew seam from top of one ear, down ear, across top of head, up second ear and across top of second ear. Insert toy filling into head – but do not stuff ears – and body through open legs, then sew up leg seams from side of one foot, around foot, up first leg, down second leg and around second foot, inserting toy filling into legs as you sew the seam. Fold each arm in half, matching row ends. Using mattress stitch, sew cast-on edges then cast-off edges together. Insert toy filling. Using chain stitch or mattress stitch as preferred, sew arms to sides of body. Using C, make a pom-pom approx. 5cm in diameter and sew to back above legs.
Embroider as follows:
The face: for each eye, using black tapestry wool and backstitch, embroider an oval with a vertical line either side of the iris area. Fill in the irises with satin stitch in blue and the areas on either side with satin stitch in white; for the mouth, using pink, embroider a cross. See also page 124.

Rita Raccoon is a workaholic; she is always checking her emails and talking on her phone, as well as looking after her two mischievous boys. Sometimes she is so busy she freezes on the spot for a few minutes — until she's off again!

Rita Raccoon

pattern

FRONT

First leg

*Using the thumb method and A, cast on 5 sts.

Row 1 and every alt row (WS): Purl.

Row 2: K1, M1R, k3, M1L, k1. (7 sts)

Row 4: K1, M1R, k5, M1L, k1. (9 sts)

Row 5: Purl.

Row 6: Knit.

Row 7: Purl.*

Row 8: K1, M1R, k to end. (10 sts)

Rows 9: Purl.

Cut yarn and put sts onto a stitch holder.

Second leg

Work as for First Leg from * to *.

Row 8: K to last st, M1L, k1. (10 sts)

Row 9: Purl.

Leave sts on needle.

Join legs

Row 10 (RS): Knit across 10 sts on needle, cast on 12 sts using the backward loop method, with RS facing knit across 10 sts from stitch holder. (32 sts)

Row 15: P9, p2tog, p10, p2togtbl, p9. (30 sts)

Starting with a k row, work 26 rows st st.

Shape arms

Row 42: K1, M1R, k to last st, M1L, k1. (32 sts)

Row 43: P1, M1L, p to last st, M1R, p1. (34 sts)

Rep rows 42–43 once more. (38 sts)

Starting with a k row, work 2 rows st st.

Row 48: K1, skpo, k to last 3 sts, k2tog, k1. (36 sts)

Row 49: P1, p2tog, p to last 3 sts, p2togtbl, p1. (34 sts)

Rep rows 48–49 once more. (30 sts)

Starting with a k row, work 8 rows st st.

Head

Join in B.

Using B, starting with a k row and stranding A up the WS right-hand edge, work 4 rows st st,

Cut B and cont in A.

Starting with a k row, work 6 rows st st.

Shape first ear

Row 70: K15, turn.

Work on this set of 15 sts only and put the rem sts on a stitch holder.

Rows 71: P1, p2tog, p to end. (14 sts)

Row 72: K to last 3 sts, k2tog, k1. (13 sts)

Rep rows 71–72 four more times. (5 sts)

Row 81: Purl.

Cast off.

Shape second ear

Put the 15 sts on stitch holder onto a needle and with RS facing, rejoin yarn.

Row 70: K15.

Rows 71: P to last 3 sts, p2togtbl, p1. (14 sts)

Row 72: K1, skpo, k to end. (13 sts)

Size

Completed creature measures approx. 23cm tall

Yarn suggestion

Lightweight yarn (such as Rowan Wool Cotton) 1 x 50g ball in A (black – Inky 908) and 1 ball in B (cream – Antique 900)

Needles

Pair of 3.25mm knitting needles

Extras

Stitch holder

Tapestry needle

Washable toy filling

Oddments of black and blue tapestry wool for embroidery

Tension

23 stitches and 35 rows to 10cm over st st using 3.25mm needles

Abbreviations

See page 126

Rep rows 71–72 four times. (5 sts)
Row 81: Purl.
Cast off.

BACK
Work as given for Front, using A only.

TAIL (make two)
Using the thumb method and A, cast on
10 sts.
Starting with a k row, work 4 rows st st.
Join in B, strand the yarn not in use up the
WS right-hand edge of the work.
Using B.
Starting with a k row, work 2 rows st st.
Row 7: K1, M1R, k to last st,
M1L, k1. (12 sts)
Row 8: Purl.
Rep rows 1–8 eight more
times. (28 sts)

Using A.
Starting with a k row, work 4 rows st st.
Using B.
Starting with a k row, work 4 rows st st.
Using A.
Starting with a k row, work 4 rows st st.
Using B.
Starting with a k row, work 4 rows st st.
Using A.
Row 89: K1, skpo, k to last 3 sts, k2tog, k1.
(26 sts)
Row 90: Purl.
Rep rows 89–90 once more. (24 sts)
Using B.
Row 93: As row 89. (22 sts)
Row 94: P1, p2tog, p to last
3 sts, p2togtbl, p1. (20 sts)
Rep rows 93–94 once more.
(16 sts)
Cut B and cont in A.
Row 97: As row 89. (14 sts)
Row 98: Purl.
Cast off.

NOSE
Using the thumb method and A,
cast on 28 sts.
Row 1 and every alt row (WS):
Purl.
Row 2: K24, short-row-wrap the next
st, turn.
Row 4: K20, short-row-wrap the next
st, turn.
Row 6: K16, short-row-wrap the next
st, turn.
Row 8: K12, short-row-wrap the next
st, turn.
Row 10: K8, short-row-wrap the next
st, turn.
Row 12: K4, short-row-wrap the next
st, turn.
Row 14: K4, [pick up the short-row-wrap
and k tog with the wrapped st, k3] six times.
Rows 15–42: Rep rows 1–14, twice.
Cast off.

TO MAKE UP
Press pieces gently following directions on
the ball band.
Using mattress stitch, sew cast-on and
cast-off edges of nose together. Insert toy
filling into nose. Using mattress stitch, sew
nose to front of head, following photograph
for position.
Using mattress stitch, sew the body pieces
together around the outer edges, weaving
loose ends into seam wherever possible and
leaving a small opening. Insert toy filling and
sew opening closed.
Using mattress stitch, sew tail pieces
together around the outer edges, leaving
the cast-on edges open. Weave in loose
ends, insert toy filling and sew cast-on
edge to back body piece, centred just above
the legs.
Embroider as follows:
The face: for each eye, working on the white
band and using black tapestry wool and
backstitch, embroider an oval with a
vertical line either side of the iris area. Fill in
the irises with satin stitch in blue; for the
nose, using black and satin stitch,
embroider over the tip of the knitted nose.
See also page 124.

Percy is a distinguished sort of dog; he sniffs out the finest
sausages and never settles for anything other than the best.
His favourite sausage at the moment is pork and
marmalade. Delicious!

Percival Long Dog

pattern

BODY, HEAD and LEGS
Using the cable method, cast on 53 sts.

Row 1 (RS): Knit.

Row 2: Purl.

Shape tail and first back leg
Row 3: Cast on 8 sts, k34, M1R, k1, M1L, k26. (63 sts)

Row 4: Cast on 8 sts, p to end. (71 sts)

Row 5: K2, M1R, k31, skpo, k1, k2tog, k31, M1L, k2. (71 sts)

Row 6: P33, p2tog, p1, p2togtbl, p33. (69 sts)

Row 7: K2, M1R, k30, skpo, k1, k2tog, k30, M1L, k2. (69 sts)

Row 8: P32, p2tog, p1, p2togtbl, p32. (67 sts)

Row 9: K2, skpo, k27, skpo, k1, k2tog, k27, k2tog, k2. (63 sts)

Row 10: P29, p2tog, p1, p2togtbl, p29. (61 sts)

Row 11: K2, skpo, k to last 4 sts, k2tog, k2. (59 sts)

Row 12: Purl.

Row 13: Cast off 8 sts, k to end. (51 sts)

Row 14: Cast off 8 sts, p to end. (43 sts)

Starting with a k row, work 4 rows st st.

Shape second back leg
Row 19: Cast on 8 sts, k to end. (51 sts)

Row 20: Cast on 8 sts, p to end. (59 sts)

Row 21: K2, M1R, k to last 2 sts, M1L, k2. (61 sts)

Row 22: Purl.

Rep rows 21–22 once more. (63 sts)

Row 25: K2, skpo, k to last 4 sts, k2tog, k2. (61 sts)

Row 26: Purl.

Rep rows 25–26 once more. (59 sts)

Row 29: Cast off 8 sts, k to end. (51 sts)

Row 30: Cast off 8 sts, p to end. (43 sts)

Body
Starting with a k row, work in st st until work measures 76cm from cast-on edge, ending with a WS row.

Shape head and first front leg
Next row: Cast on 8 sts, k to end. (51 sts)

Next row: Cast on 8 sts, p to end. (59 sts)

Next row: K2, M1R, k27, M1R, k1, M1L, k27, M1L, k2. (63 sts)

Next row and foll 3 alt rows: Purl.

Next row: K2, M1R, k28, M1R, k3, M1L, k28, M1L, k2. (67 sts)

Next row: K2, skpo, k28, M1R, k3, M1L, k28, k2tog, k2. (67 sts)

Next row: K2, skpo, k28, M1R, k3, M1L, k28, k2tog, k2. (67 sts)
Next row: Cast off 8 sts, k23, M1R, k3, M1L, k32. (61 sts)
Next row: Cast off 8 sts, p to end. (53 sts)
Next row: K25, M1R, k3, M1L, k25. (55 sts)
Starting with a p row, work 3 rows st st.

Shape head and second front leg
Next row: Cast on 8 sts, k to end. (63 sts)
Next row: Cast on 8 sts, p to end. (71 sts)
Next row: K2, M1R, k30, skpo, k3, k2tog, k30, M1L, k2. (71 sts)
Next row and foll 3 alt rows: Purl.
Next row: K2, M1R, k30, skpo, k3, k2tog, k30, M1L, k2. (71 sts)
Next row: K2, skpo, k28, skpo, k3, k2tog, k28, k2tog, k2. (67 sts)
Next row: K2, skpo, k26, skpo, k3, k2tog, k26, k2tog, k2. (63 sts)
Cast off 8 sts, k20, skpo, k1, k2tog, k29. (53 sts)
Cast off 8 sts, p to end. (45 sts)
Next row: K2, skpo, k16, skpo, k1, k2tog, k16, k2tog, k2. (41 sts)
Next row: Purl.
Next row: K2, skpo, k2, skpo, k10, skpo, k1, k2tog, k10, k2tog, k2, k2tog, k2. (35 sts)
Next row: P2, p2tog, p to last 4 sts, p2togtbl, p2. (33 sts)

Next row: K2, skpo, k2, skpo, k6, skpo, k1, k2tog, k6, k2tog, k2, k2tog, k2. (27 sts)
Next row: P2, p2tog, p to last 4 sts, p2togtbl, p2. (25 sts)
Next row: K2, skpo, k6, skpo, k1, k2tog, k6, k2tog, k2. (21 sts)
Starting with a p row, work 9 rows st st.

Shape nose
Next row: K2, skpo, k4, skpo, k1, k2tog, k4, k2tog, k2. (17 sts)
Next row: P2, p2tog, p2, p2tog, p1, p2togtbl, p2, p2togtbl, p2. (13 sts)
Cast off.

EARS (both together)
Using thumb method, cast on 51 sts.
Row 1: [K1, p1] rep to last st, k1.
Row 1 establishes moss st.
Rep row 1 once more.
Row 3: [K1, p1] twice, k1, M1R, k to last 5 sts, M1L, [k1, p1] twice, k1. (53 sts)
Row 4: [K1, p1] twice, p to last 3 sts, k1, p1, k1.
Rep rows 3–4 once more. (55 sts)
Row 7: [K1, p1] twice, k1, skpo, k to last 7 sts, k2tog, [k1, p1] twice, k1. (53 sts)
Row 8: [K1, p1] twice, p to last 3 sts, k1, p1, k1.
Rep rows 7–8 once more. (51 sts)

Row 11: [K1, p1] rep to last st, k1.
Rep row 11 once more.
Cast off in moss.

TO MAKE UP
Press knitted pieces following instructions on the ball band.
Fold knitting in half lengthways, matching legs. Pleat centre of ears and sew to head, following photograph for position.
Using mattress stitch, sew body together along lower edges, weaving loose ends into the seam wherever possible. Insert toy filling as you sew.
Embroider as follows:
The face: for each eye, using black tapestry wool and backstitch, embroider an oval with a vertical line either side of the iris area. Fill in the irises with satin stitch in blue and the areas on either side with satin stitch in white; for the nose, using black and satin stitch, embroider an inverted triangle on the end of the knitted nose; for the moustache, using black and backstitch, embroider a curl on each cheek. See also page 124.

Size

Completed cupcake measures approx.
20cm tall

Yarn suggestion

Lightweight yarn (such as Rowan
Cotton Glacé) 1 x 50g ball in
A (white – Bleached 726), 1 ball in
D (pink – Bubbles 724)

Lightweight yarn (such as Rowan
Wool Cotton) 1 x 50g ball in
B (brown – Bronze 967), 1 ball in
C (pale pink – Tender 951)

Fine-weight yarn (such as Rowan
4 ply Soft) 1 x 50g ball in
E (red – Honk 374)

Needles

Set of four double-pointed 3mm
knitting needles

Extras

Round marker

Tapestry needle

Washable toy filling

Tension

25 stitches and 33 rows to 10cm over
st st using 3mm needles

Abbreviations

See page 126

Completely fat-free, this cupcake can definitely be snacked upon between meals. Ice it with yellow yarn if you prefer a lemon fancy or pink yarn for a strawberry parfait.

Giant Cupcake

pattern

CUPCAKE

Icing

Using the thumb method and A, cast on 6 sts onto one needle.

Round 1 (RS): To start working in the round, slip half the stitches onto a second needle and position the two needles side by side with the first cast-on stitch and the last cast-on stitch adjacent on separate needles. Use a third needle to start knitting the round starting with the first cast-on stitch and working two stitches. Use a fourth needle to knit the next two stitches, one from each of the original two needles. (2 sts on each needle.) Complete knitting the round with the needle that has now become free. Place round marker at the start of the round.

Round 2: [Inc] six times.
(4 sts on each needle)

Round 3: Knit.

Round 4: [K1, M1R] twelve times.
(8 sts on each needle)

Round 5: Knit.

Round 6: [K2, M1R] twelve times.
(12 sts on each needle)

Round 7: Knit.

Round 8: [K3, M1R] twelve times.
(16 sts on each needle)

Rounds 9–10: Knit.

Round 11: [K4, M1R] twelve times.
(20 sts on each needle)

Rounds 12–13: Knit.

Round 14: [K5, M1R] twelve times.
(24 sts on each needle)
Knit 4 rounds.
Cut A and join in B.

Cake
Knit 20 rounds.

Round 39: [K4, skpo, k4, k2tog] six times.
(20 sts on each needle)
Cut B and join in C and D.

Case

Round 40: [K1C, k1D] rep to end of round.
Rep round 40 twenty-three more times.
Using D, knit 2 rounds.
Cut D.

Base
Work in C only.
Purl 3 rounds.
Weave in loose ends and insert toy filling.

Round 69: [K3, k2tog] twelve times.
(16 sts on each needle)

Round 70: Purl.

Round 71: Knit.

Round 72: Purl.

Round 73: [K2, k2tog] twelve times.
(12 sts on each needle)

Round 74: Purl.

Round 75: Knit.

Round 76: Purl.
Insert toy filling.

Round 77: [K1, k2tog] twelve times.
(8 sts on each needle)

Round 78: Purl.

Round 79: Knit.

Round 80: Purl.

Round 81: [K2tog] twelve times.
(4 sts on each needle)

Round 82: Purl.
Cut C 10cm from the last stitch on the needle and thread onto a tapestry needle. Pass the tapestry needle through all the stitches on the needles in the order they would have been knitted, use the tip of the needle to pull the yarn at the point just after it has passed through the first stitch to draw the stitches tight to the yarn, then pull the yarn tight as it emerges through the last stitch. Secure the end.

CHERRY

Using the thumb method and E, cast on 12 sts.

Row 1 (WS): Purl.

Row 2: Knit.

Rows 3-16: Rep rows 1–2 seven times or until the knitted piece is a square.
Cast off.

TO MAKE UP

Form the cherry by working a line of running stitches around the four sides of the square piece, placing some toy filling in the centre, drawing the stitches up tight and securing the end. Sew the cherry to the top of the cupcake.

Mimi Mushroom is by far the best at hide-and-seek among the trees. She is small and quiet and can stay still for a long time.

Mimi Mushroom

pattern

FRONT

First leg

Using the thumb method, cast on 5 sts.

Row 1 (WS): Purl.

Row 2: K1, M1R, k to end. (6 sts)

Row 3: Purl.

Rep rows 2–3 three more times. (9 sts)

Row 10: K1, M1R, k5, k2tog, k1. (9 sts)

Row 11: Purl.

Row 12: As row 10.

Row 13. Purl.

Cut yarn and put sts onto stitch holder.

Second leg

Using the thumb method, cast on 5 sts.

Row 1 (WS): Purl.

Row 2: K1, M1R, k3, M1L, k1. (7 sts)

Row 3: Purl.

Row 4: Knit.

Row 5: Purl.

Leave sts on needle and do not cut yarn.

Join legs

Row 14: Knit across 7 sts on needles, cast on 3 sts using the backward loop method, with RS facing knit across 6 sts from stitch holder, k2tog, k1. (18 sts)

Body

Row 15: P7, p2tog, p1, p2togtbl, p6. (16 sts)

Starting with a k row, work 9 rows st st.

Skirt ridge

Rows 25–27: Knit.

Starting with a k row, work 10 rows st st.

Shape arms

Row 38: K1, M1R, k to end. (17 sts)

Row 39: Cast on 2 sts using the backward loop method, p to end. (19 sts)

Row 40: Knit.

Row 41: P1, M1L, p to end. (20 sts)

Row 42: K1, M1R, k to end. (21 sts)

Row 43: P1, p2tog, p to last st, M1R, p1.

Row 44: K1, M1R, k to end. (22 sts)

Row 45: Cast off 2 sts, p to end. (20 sts)

Row 46: K1, skpo, k to last 3 sts, k2tog, k1. (18 sts)

Row 47: Purl.

Row 48: K1, skpo, k to end. (17 sts)

Row 49: Purl.

Row 50: K1, skpo, k to last st, M1L, k1.

Row 51: Purl.

Row 52: K to last st, M1L, K1. (18 sts)

Rep rows 51–52 once more. (19 sts)

Row 55: Purl.

Row 56: K1, M1R, k to last st, M1L, k1. (21 sts)

Rep rows 55–56 once more. (23 sts)

Shape top

Row 59: Cast on 4 sts using the backward loop method, p to end. (27 sts)

Row 60: Cast on 7 sts using the backward loop method, k to end. (34 sts)

Row 61: Purl.

Row 62: K1, skpo, k to end. (33 sts)

Row 63: Purl.

Row 64: Knit.

Row 65: Purl.

Row 66: K1, skpo, k to end. (32 sts)

Starting with a p row, work 3 rows st st.

Row 70: K1, skpo, k to last 3 sts, k2tog, k1. (30 sts)

Row 71: Purl.

Row 72: K to last 3 sts, k2tog, k1. (29 sts)

Row 73: Purl.

Rep rows 70–73 twice more. (23 sts)

Row 82: K1, skpo, k to last 3 sts, k2tog, k1. (21 sts)

Row 83: Purl.

Rep rows 82–83 once more. (19 sts)

Row 86: K1, skpo, k to last 3 sts, k2tog, k1. (17 sts)

Row 87: P1, p2tog, p to last 3 sts, p2togtbl, p1. (15 sts)

Rep rows 86–87 once more. (11 sts)

Cast off.

BACK

Work as given for Front, reversing RS of work (to make a mirrored pair of pieces) by reading knit for purl and vice versa. See page 118 for reverse shaping tips.

TO MAKE UP

Press pieces gently following directions on the ball band.

Using mattress stitch, sew body pieces together around the outer edges, leaving a small opening. Insert toy filling and sew opening closed.

Embroider as follows:

The face: for each eye, using black tapestry wool and backstitch, embroider an oval. Using satin stitch, embroider a wide black central stripe for the irises and fill in the areas on either side with satin stitch in white; for the eyebrows, using black and backstitch, embroider a line above each eye; for the mouth, using black and backstitch, embroider the opening and outline the teeth. Fill in the mouth with satin stitch in orange. For the cheeks, using backstitch and orange, embroider circles. See also page 124.

Robin is a soft and gentle bird. He teaches sky-diving to beginners but has to watch his weight as he is partial to a worm or two!

Size
Completed creature measures approx. 17cm tall, excluding legs

Yarn suggestion
Lightweight yarn (such as Debbie Bliss Rialto) 1 x 50g ball in
A (red – 12), 1 ball in
B (brown – 05) and 1 ball in
C (pink – 13)

Needles
Pair of 3.25mm knitting needles

Extras
Tapestry needle

Washable toy filling

Scrap of cream felt

Sewing needle and thread to match felt

Oddments of black, green and white tapestry wool for embroidery

Tension
24 stitches and 34 rows to 10cm over st st using 3.25mm needles

Abbreviations
See page 126

Robin Red Breast

pattern

Note: decrease (dec) using k2tog if second stitch of two being worked together is a knit stitch or p2tog if it is a purl stitch.

FRONT

Using the cable method and A, cast on 30 sts.
Row 1 (RS): Knit.
Row 2: Purl.

Shape tummy

Row 3: K2, M1R, k to last 2 sts, M1L, k2. (32 sts)
Row 4: Purl.
Rep rows 3–4 five more times. (42 sts)
Starting with a k row, work 22 rows st st.
Cast off.

Shape head

Using B, pick up 42 sts across cast-off edge.
Next row: Purl.
*Next row: [P2, k2] rep to last 2 sts, p2.
Next row: [K2, p2] rep to last 2 sts, k2.
Rep last 2 rows three more times.
Next row: [P2, k2] rep to last 2 sts, p2.
Next row: Dec, rib as set to last 2 sts, dec. (40 sts)
Rib 3 rows as set.
Rep last 4 rows once more. (38 sts)
Next row: Dec, rib as set to last 2 sts, dec. (36 sts)
Rib 1 row as set.
Rep last 2 rows three more times. (30 sts)
Next row: Dec, rib as set to last 2 sts, dec.
Rep last row five more times. (18 sts)
Cast off.*

BACK

Using the cable method and B, cast on 30 sts.
Row 1 (RS): [K2, p2] rep to last 2 sts, k2.
Row 2: [P2, k2] rep to last 2 sts, p2.
Row 3: Cast on 2 sts, [p2, k2] rep to end. (32 sts)
Row 4: Cast on 2 sts, [k2, p2] rep to last 2 sts, k2. (34 sts)

Row 5: [P2, k2] rep to last 2 sts, p2.
Row 6: [K2, p2] rep to last 2 sts, k2.
Row 7: Cast on 2 sts, [k2, p2] rep to end. (36 sts)
Row 8: Cast on 2 sts, [p2, k2] rep to last 2 sts, p2. (38 sts)
Row 9: [K2, p2] rep to last 2 sts, k2.
Row 10: [P2, k2] rep to last 2 sts, p2.
Row 11: Cast on 3 sts, p3, [k2, p2] rep to last 2 sts, k2. (41 sts)
Row 12: Cast on 3 sts, k3, [p2, k2] rep to last 5 sts, p2, k3. (44 sts)
Row 13: P3, [k2, p2] rep to last 5 sts, k2, p3.
Row 14: K3, [p2, k2] rep to last 5 sts, p2, k3.
Rep rows 13–14 ten more times.
Row 35: As row 13.
Row 36: Dec, k1, [p2, k2] rep to last 5 sts, p2, k1, dec. (42 sts)
Rep from * to * of Front.

WINGS (make two)

Using the thumb method and B, cast on 9 sts.
Row 1 (WS): [K1, p1] rep to last st , k1.
Rep row 1 twice more.
Row 4: K1, p1, k1, M1R, k to last 3 sts, M1L, k1, p1, k1. (11 sts)
Row 5: K1, p to last st, k1.
Rep rows 4–5 twice more. (15 sts)
Row 10: K1, p1, k to last 2 sts, p1, k1.
Row 11: K1, p to last st, k1.
Rep rows 10–11 five more times.
Row 22: K1, p1, k1, skpo, k to last 5 sts, k2tog, k1, p1, k1. (13 sts)
Row 23: K1, p to last st, k1.
Rep rows 22–23 twice more. (9 sts)
Row 28: K1, p1, k1, s2tog, k1, psso, k1, p1, k1. (7 sts)
Row 29: K1, p to last st, k1.
Row 30: K1, p1, s2tog, k1, psso, p1, k1. (5 sts)
Row 31: [K1, p1] twice, k1.
Rep row 31 twice more.
Row 34: K1, p3tog, k1. (3 sts)

Row 35: K1, p1, k1.
Rep row 35 four more times.
Cut yarn leaving a long tail. Pass yarn through rem 3 sts and pull up tight.

FEET (make two)

Using the cable method and C, cast on 18 sts.
*Cast off 5 sts, slip st on right-hand needle onto left-hand needle.
Cast on 5 sts.*
Rep from * to *.
Cast off 18 sts.

WORM (optional)

Using the cable method and C, cast on 40 sts loosely.
Cast off all sts tightly.

TO MAKE UP

Press knitted pieces following instructions on ball band. Weave in loose ends neatly. Using mattress stitch and working one stitch in from the edge, sew body pieces together around the outer edges, leaving a small opening. Insert toy filling and sew opening closed. Sew legs to lower edge of body, following photograph for position. Position cast-on edge of each wing at an angle on sides of body. Using slip stitch, sew front and top edges of wings to body, leaving wings tips free. Bend wings up.
Cut felt into a diamond, fold in half and position on face for beak. Using sewing needle and thread, sew across middle of diamond to sew to head. Sew worm into beak.
Embroider as follows:
The face: for each eye, using black tapestry wool and backstitch, embroider an oval with a vertical line either side of the iris area. Fill in the irises with satin stitch in green and the areas on either side with satin stitch in white. See also page 124.

Deirdre is by far the most glamorous of the creatures. Her favourite pastime is shopping for new wings; she always goes to designer wing shops and picks out pairs in this season's colours.

Deidre Dragonfly

pattern

Note: to prepare for beading, thread sewing cotton through a fine needle and tie to A, then pass the needle through the beads and slide them down the yarn.

BODY and HEAD

Tail

Using four 3mm double-pointed needles, the thumb method and A, cast on 6 sts onto one needle.

Round 1 (RS): To start working in the round, slip half the stitches onto a second needle and position the two needles side by side with the first cast-on stitch and the last cast-on stitch adjacent on separate needles. Use a third needle to start knitting the round starting with the first cast-on stitch and working two stitches. Use a fourth needle to knit the next two stitches, one from each of the original two needles. (2 sts on each needle.) Complete knitting the round with the needle that has now become free.

Round 2: [Inc] six times.
(4 sts on each needle)
Arrange sts over four needles.
(3 sts on each needle)
Place round marker at the start of the round. Starting with a knit (RS) round, place beads as indicated by the chart. The first and third needles hold the side stitches, the second and fourth needles hold the front and back

stitches – those on which beading and shaping occur. Work shaping as follows:

Rounds 3–4 (RS): Knit 2 rounds.

Round 5: K3 on first/third needle, k1, M1R, k1, M1L, k1 on second/fourth needle. (3 sts on first needle, 5 sts on second, 3 sts on third, 5 sts on fourth)

Rounds 6–7: Knit 2 rounds.

Round 8: K3 on first/third needle, work as chart as follows: k1, M1R, k1, PB, k1, M1L, k1 on second/fourth needle. (3 sts on first needle, 7 sts on second, 3 sts on third, 7 sts on fourth)

Round 9: Knit one round.

Round 10: K3 on first/third needle, work as chart as follows: k1, PB, k3, PB, k1 on second/fourth needle.
Cont beading as indicated by chart on the second and fourth needles.

Rounds 11–44: Knit 34 rounds.

Round 45: K3 on first/third needle, k1, M1R, k1, PB, k1, PB, k1, M1L, k1 on second/fourth needle. (3 sts on first needle, 9 sts on second, 3 sts on third, 9 sts on fourth)

Rounds 46–86: Knit 41 rounds.

Round 87: K3 on first/third needle, k1, M1R, PB, k5, PB, M1L, k1 on second/fourth needle. (3 sts on first needle, 11 sts on second, 3 sts on third, 11 sts on fourth)

Size

Completed creature measures approx. 40cm long

Yarn suggestion

Lightweight yarn (such as Debbie Bliss Baby Cashmerino) 1 x 50g ball in A (green – 340016) and 1 ball in B (gold – 340025)

Bead suggestion

4mm round beads (such as Miracle Bead) 238 iridescent purple beads

Needles

Set of five double-pointed 3mm knitting needles

Pair of 3mm knitting needles

Extras

Round marker

Waste cotton yarn

Tapestry needle

Washable toy filling

Oddments of black, blue and white tapestry wool for embroidery

Tension

26 stitches and 46 rows to 10cm over st st using 3mm needles

Abbreviations

See page 126

Rounds 88–122: Knit 35 rounds.
Insert toy filling.

Round 123: K3 on first/third needle, k1, skpo, k5, k2tog, k1 on second/fourth needle. (3 sts on first needle, 9 sts on second, 3 sts on third, 9 sts on fourth)

Rounds 124–126: Knit 3 rounds.

Round 127: K3 on first/third needle, k1, skpo, k3, k2tog, k1 on second/fourth needle. (3 sts on first needle, 7 sts on second, 3 sts on third, 7 sts on fourth)

Rounds 128–132: Knit 5 rounds.

Round 133: K3 on first/third needle, k1, skpo, PB, k2tog, k1 on second/fourth needle. (3 sts on first needle, 5 sts on second, 3 sts on third, 5 sts on fourth)

Round 134: Knit one round.
Chart completed.
Insert toy filling.

Head

Rounds 135–136: Knit 2 rounds.

Round 137: K3 on first/third needle, k1, M1R, k3, M1L, k1 on second/fourth needle. (3 sts on first needle, 7 sts on second, 3 sts on third, 7 sts on fourth)

Round 138: K3 on first/third needle, k1, M1R, k5, M1L, k1 on second/fourth needle. (3 sts on first needle, 9 sts on second, 3 sts on third, 9 sts on fourth)

Rounds 139–140: Knit 2 rounds.

Round 141: K3 on first/third needle, k1, M1R, k7, M1L, k1 on second/fourth needle. (3 sts on first needle, 11 sts on second, 3 sts on third, 11 sts on fourth)

Rounds 142–152: Knit 11 rounds.

Round 153: K1, k2tog on first/third needle, k2, k2tog, k1, k2tog, k2, k2tog on second/fourth needle. (2 sts on first needle, 8 sts on second, 2 sts on third, 8 sts on fourth)

Rounds 154–155: Knit 2 rounds.
Insert toy filling.

Round 156: K2tog on first/third needle, [k2tog] four times on second/fourth needle. (1 sts on first needle, 4 sts on second, 1 sts on third, 4 sts on fourth)

Round 157: Knit 1 round.
Cut A 10cm from the last stitch on the needle and thread into a tapestry needle. Pass the tapestry needle through all the stitches on the needles in the order they would have been knitted, use the tip of the needle to pull the yarn at the point just after it has passed through the first stitch to draw the stitches tight to the yarn, then pull the yarn tight as it emerges through the last stitch. Secure the end.

LARGER WINGS (make two)
Using 3mm needles, the thumb method and B, cast on 10 sts.

Row 1: K1tbl, [p1, k1] four times, bring yarn forward between the needles, sl1 purlwise
Rep row 1 three more times.

Row 5: K1tbl, inc, [p1, k1] three times, inc, bring yarn forward between the needles, sl1 purlwise. (12 sts)

Row 6: K1tbl, inc, [p1, k1] four times, inc, bring yarn forward between the needles, sl1 purlwise. (14 sts)

Row 7: K1tbl, [k1, p1] six times, bring yarn forward between the needles, sl1 purlwise.

Row 8: K1tbl, inc, [k1, p1] five times, inc, bring yarn forward between the needles, sl1 purlwise. (16 sts)

Row 9: K1tbl, [p1, k1] seven times, bring yarn forward between the needles, sl1 purlwise.

Row 10: K1tbl, inc, [p1, k1] six times, inc, bring yarn forward between the needles, sl1 purlwise. (18 sts)

Row 11: K1tbl, [k1, p1] eight times, bring yarn forward between the needles, sl1 purlwise.

Row 12: K1tbl, [p1, k1] eight times, bring yarn forward between the needles, sl1 purlwise.

Row 13: Rep row 11.

Row 14: K1tbl, inc, [k1, p1] seven times, inc, bring yarn forward between the needles, sl1 purlwise. (20 sts)

Row 15: K1tbl, [p1, k1] nine times, bring yarn forward between the needles, sl1 purlwise.

Row 16: K1tbl, [k1, p1] nine times, bring yarn forward between the needles, sl1 purlwise.
Rep rows 15–16 nine more times.

Row 35: K1tbl, skpo, [p1, k1] seven times, k2tog, bring yarn forward between the needles, sl1 purlwise. (18 sts)

Row 36: K1tbl, skpo, [p1, k1] six times, k2tog, bring yarn forward between the needles, sl1 purlwise.
(16 sts)
Cast off as follows: Skpo, k1, pass the first st loop on the right-hand needle over the second, cont to cast off keeping the moss st patt correct until 2 sts rem on the left-hand needle, k2tog, pass the first st loop on the right-hand needle over the second.
Fasten off.

SMALLER WINGS (make two)
Using 3mm needles, the thumb method and B, cast on 10 sts.

Row 1: K1tbl, [p1, k1] four times, bring yarn forward between the needles, sl1 purlwise
Rep row 1 three more times.

Row 5: K1tbl, inc, [p1, k1] three times, inc, bring yarn forward between the needles, sl1 purlwise. (12 sts)

Row 6: K1tbl, [k1, p1] five times, bring yarn forward between the needles, sl1 purlwise.

Row 7: K1tbl, [p1, k1] five times, bring yarn forward between the needles, sl1 purlwise.
Rep rows 6–7 fourteen more times.

Row 36: K1tbl, skpo, [k1, p1] three times, k2tog, bring yarn forward between the needles, sl1 purlwise. (10 sts)
Cast off as follows: Skpo, p1, pass the first st loop on the right-hand needle over the second, cont to cast off keeping the moss st patt correct until 2 sts rem on the left-hand needle, k2tog, pass the first st loop on the right-hand needle over the second.
Fasten off.

TO MAKE UP

Press pieces gently following directions on the ball band.

Using whip stitch, sew the wings to the sides of the body, following photograph for position.

Embroider as follows:

The face: for each eye, using black tapestry wool and backstitch, embroider an oval with a vertical line either side of the iris area. Fill in the irises with satin stitch in blue and the areas on either side with satin stitch in white; for the mouth, using black and satin stitch, embroider a smile. Cut a strand of yarn B 24cm long and thread into needle. Take yarn through head above each eye to form two antenna. See also page 124.

BODY

A

PB

You will find Titi Toadstool hanging out with Mimi Mushroom deep in the cardboard forest. They play hide-and-seek but usually Titi gets found first as she can't keep quiet for long.

Titi Toadstool

pattern

FRONT

Legs

Using the thumb method and A, cast on 24 sts.

Row 1 (WS): Purl.

Row 2: K1, M1R, k10, M1R, k2, M1L, k10, M1L, k1. (28 sts)

Row 3: P1, M1L, p12, M1L, p2, M1R, p12, M1R, p1. (32 sts)

Row 4: K1, M1R, k14, M1R, k2, M1L, k14, M1L, k1. (36 sts)

Row 5: P17, M1L, p2, M1R, p17. (38 sts)

Row 6: K1, M1R, k17, M1R, k2, M1L, k17, M1L, k1. (42 sts)

Row 7: P20, M1L, p2, M1R, p20. (44 sts)

Row 8: K1, skpo, k18, M1R, k2, M1L, k18, k2tog, k1.

Row 9: P21, M1L, p2, M1R, p21. (46 sts)

Row 10: K1, skpo, k19, M1R, k2, M1L, k19, k2tog, k1.

Row 11: P1, p2tog, p19, M1L, p2, M1R, p19, p2togtbl, p1.

Row 12: As row 10.

Row 13: Cast off purlwise as follows: p2tog, p1, pass the first st loop on the right-hand needle over the second, cont to cast off 8 more sts, p23, cast off 9 sts, p2togtbl, pass the first st loop on the right-hand needle over the second. Fasten off. (24 sts) Cut yarn.

Stalk

With RS facing, rejoin A.

Starting with a k row, work 24 rows st st.

Arms

Row 38: K1, M1R, k to last st, M1L, k1. (26 sts)

Row 39: P1, M1L, p to last st, M1R, p1. (28 sts)

Rep rows 38–39 once more. (32 sts)

Starting with a k row, work 2 rows st st.

Row 44: K1, skpo, k to last 3 sts, k2tog, k1. (30 sts)

Row 45: P1, p2tog, p to last 3 sts, p2togtbl, p1. (28 sts)

Rep rows 44–45 once more. (24 sts)

Starting with a k row, work 24 rows st st.

Cap

Join in B. Starting with a knit (RS) row, working in Fair Isle, stranding the yarn not in use on the WS and weaving in yarn as required, work colour patt from the chart. Work shaping as follows:

Rows 72–81: Work 10 rows st st. Cut yarns A and B.

Row 82: Using the thumb method and B, cast on 12 sts, work across row 82 of the chart, cast on 12 sts using the backward loop method. (48 sts)

Rows 83–99: Starting with a p row, work 17 rows st st.

Row 100: K1, skpo, k to last 3 sts, k2tog, k1. (46 sts)

Rows 101–105: Starting with a p row, work 5 rows st st.

Row 106: K1, skpo, k to last 3 sts, k2tog, k1. (44 sts)

Rows 107–109: Starting with a p row, work 3 rows st st.

Size

Completed creature measures approx. 36cm tall

Yarn suggestion

Lightweight yarn (such as Debbie Bliss Rialto) 2 x 50g balls in A (white – 23001) and 1 ball in B (red – 23012)

Needles

Pair of 3.75mm knitting needles

Other materials

Tapestry needle

Washable toy filling

Oddments of black, blue and white tapestry wool for embroidery

Tension

24 stitches and 38 rows to 10cm over st st using 3.75mm needles

Abbreviations

See page 126

Rows 110–113: Rep rows 106–109 once. (42 sts)

Row 114: K1, skpo, k to last 3 sts, k2tog, k1. (40 sts)

Row 115: Purl.

Rows 116–119: Rep rows 114–115 twice. (36 sts)

Row 120: K1, skpo, k to last 3 sts, k2tog, k1. (34 sts)

Row 121: P1, p2tog, p to last 3 sts, p2togtbl, p1. (32 sts)

Rows 122–123: Rep rows 120–121 once. (28 sts)

Row 124: K1 [skpo] twice, k to last 5 sts, [k2tog] twice, k1. (24 sts)

Row 125: P1 [p2tog] twice, p to last 5 sts, [p2togtbl] twice, p1. (20 sts)

Row 126: K1 [skpo] twice, k to last 5 sts, [k2tog] twice, k1. (16 sts)

Row 127: Cast off 4 sts purlwise, p11. (12 sts)

Row 128: Cast off 4 sts knitwise, k7. (8 sts) Cast off.

BACK

Work as given for Front, reversing RS of work (to make a mirrored pair of pieces) by reading knit for purl and vice versa. See page 118 for reverse shaping tips.

TO MAKE UP

Press pieces gently following directions on the ball band.

Using mattress stitch, sew the body pieces together around the outer edges, weaving loose ends into seam wherever possible and leaving a small opening. Insert toy filling and sew opening closed.

Embroider as follows:

The face: for each eye, using black tapestry wool and backstitch, embroider an oval with a vertical line either side of the iris area. Fill in the irises with satin stitch in blue and the areas on either side with satin stitch in white; for the mouth, using black and satin stitch, embroider a smile on the lowest central white spot. See also page 124.

A

B

[0] Cast on stitches in B

Peggy Long Legs

Peggy has the longest legs ever, they just keep growing. She's about one meter tall and only five years old: imagine how tall she will be when she's 30! Peggy's favourite pastime is knitting and she's the fastest knitter in the world.

pattern

FRONT

Head
*Using 4mm needles and the thumb method, cast on 24 sts.
Row 1 (WS): Purl.
Row 2: K1, M1R, k22, M1L, k1. (26 sts)
Row 3: Purl.
Row 4: K1, M1R, k24, M1L, k1. (28 sts)
Row 5: Purl.
Row 6: Knit.
Starting with a p row, work 5 rows st st.
Row 12: K1, skpo, k to last 3 sts, k2tog, k1. (26 sts)
Row 13: Purl.
Rep rows 12–13 four more times.
Starting with a k row, work 4 rows st st.

Shape arms
Row 26: Cast on 3 sts using the backward loop method, k to end. (21 sts)
Row 27: Cast on 3 sts using the backward loop method, p to end. (24 sts)
Row 28: K1, M1R, k to end. (25 sts)
Row 29: P1, M1L, p to end. (26 sts)
Row 30: K1, skpo, k to end. (25 sts)
Row 31: P1, p2tog, p to end. (24 sts)
Row 32: Cast off 3 sts, k to end. (21 sts)
Row 33: Cast off 3 sts, p to end. (18 sts)

Body
Starting with a k row, work 28 rows st st.
Row 62: K5, k2tog, k1, cast off 2 sts, skpo, k5. (7 sts on each needle)
Cut yarn* and put sts onto a stitch holder.

BACK
Starting with a new ball of yarn, work as given for Front from * to *, reversing RS of work (to make a mirrored pair of pieces) by reading knit for purl and vice versa. See page 118 for reverse shaping tips.

LEGS
Place Front and Back pieces WS together. Select one group of 7 sts on front and group of 7 sts opposite on back and put both groups of 7 sts onto two separate double-pointed needles. Put the remaining stitches of the other two groups of 7 sts onto a length of waste cotton yarn or two large safety pins.

First leg
**Join yarn to the outer edge.
Round 1: To start working in the round, use a third needle to k2tog, k3, use a fourth needle to k4, two from each of the original two needles. Use the needle that has now become free to k3, skpo. (4 sts on each needle.) Place round marker at the start of the round.
Knit 289 rounds.
Loop a short length of waste yarn through a stitch loop on the last round as a marker.**
Put all stitches onto a length of waste cotton yarn.
Do not cut yarn. **

Second leg
Put the remaining two groups of 7 sts on the stitch holders onto two separate double-pointed needles.
Rep as for First Leg from ** to **.

Both legs
Compare the amount of yarn rem in each ball of yarn.
Transferring stitches from waste yarn as necessary, cont to knit rounds on the leg with the least amount of yarn rem until 30cm of yarn rem.
Count the number of additional rounds from the marker on row 290.
***Next round:** [K2tog] six times. (6 sts)
Next round: Knit.
Cut yarn 10cm from the last stitch on the needle and thread into a tapestry needle. Pass the tapestry needle through all the stitches on the needles in the order they would have been knitted, use the tip of the needle to pull the yarn at the point just after it has passed through the first stitch to draw the stitches tight to the yarn, then pull the

yarn tight as it emerges through the last
stitch. Secure the end. ***
Transfer stitches for other leg from waste
yarn to needles.
Knit rounds equal to those of the additional
rounds on the completed leg.
Rep from *** to ***.

TO MAKE UP
Press pieces gently following directions on
the ball band.
Note that the legs are not stuffed.
Using mattress stitch, sew body pieces
together around the outer edges, weaving
loose ends into seam wherever possible and
leaving a small opening. Insert toy filling and
sew opening closed.
Embroider as follows:
The face: for each eye, using black tapestry
wool and backstitch, embroider an oval with
a vertical line either side of the iris area. Fill
in the irises with satin stitch in green and the
areas on either side with satin stitch in
white; for the eyebrows, using black and
backstitch, embroider a line above each eye;
for the mouth, using black and backstitch,
embroider an opening and outline the
teeth. Fill in the teeth with satin stitch in
white; for the cheeks, using satin stitch and
pale pink, embroider circles either side of
the mouth. See also page 124.

Knitting Equipment

Here are items of the basic equipment you will need to knit the odd-bod bunch.

Above: knitting needles come in various sizes and materials; left to right, bamboo, metal and plastic. Each pattern gives the size of the needles you need, but the type of needle is up to you. Beginners might find bamboo needles easiest to use as they aren't as smooth as the others so stitches don't tend to slip off unexpectedly.

Above: double-pointed knitting needles have a point at each end. This allows you to knit from either end and so knit in the round.

Above: the cable needle shown is a cranked one, which will hold the stitches safely while you work the cable.

Above: stitch holders are used to keep some stitches separate while you work on another part of the project.

Above: when you are working colour knitting, wind lengths of the yarns onto separate bobbins and knit from these to avoid tangling up your balls of yarn.

Above: tapestry needles have a blunt point to help prevent them splitting the yarn when you are sewing up a project.

Above: there are various types of round marker, from metal rings to pretty, beaded ones. However, you can just use a loop of contrast-colour yarn.

Knitting Techniques

If you are a novice knitter, these pages will show you how to get started so that you can knit members of the odd-bod bunch. Once you've mastered the basics, you'll also find instructions for more advanced techniques that feature in some of the creatures.

holding yarn and needles

There is no right or wrong way of holding the yarn and needles, so try these popular methods and use whichever feels most comfortable.

In the UK and USA the left-hand needle is usually held from above, like a knife, and the right-hand needle in the crook of your thumb, like a pen. The working end of the yarn (the end attached to the ball) goes over your right index finger, under your second finger and over your ring finger to help control the tension of the stitches. Your right index finger moves back and forth to wind the yarn around the tip of the right-hand needle.

The other method, often called the 'continental method', also holds the right-hand needle like a pen, but the left-hand needle is held between your thumb and second finger. The working yarn goes over your left index finger, under your second and ring fingers and over your little finger to control the tension. Your left index finger is held aloft and moves back and forth to wind the yarn around the tip of the right-hand needle.

slip knot

The starting point for any piece of knitting is a slip knot.

1 Lay the tail end of the yarn over the ball end to form a loop.

2 Bring the tail end under the ball end and across the back of the loop of yarn. Slip the tip of a knitting needle under this tail end.

3 Pull on both ends of the yarn and the slip knot will tighten around the needle. This knot will always be the first cast on stitch.
After you have knitted the first couple of rows, you can pull gently on the tail end of the yarn to tighten the first stitch if it is a bit loose.

thumb cast on

This cast on involves using just one knitting needle and your left thumb and produces an elastic edge. If you are working with double-knitting yarn, making a slip knot about 50cm from the end will allow you to cast on about 40 stitches.

1 Make a slip knot the required distance from the end of the yarn. Hold the needle with the knot on in your right hand. *Wind the tail end of the yarn (the end not attached to the ball) clockwise around your left thumb.

2 Put the tip of the needle under the front of the loop of yarn around your thumb.

3 With your right index finger, wind the ball end of the yarn around the tip of the needle, taking it between the needle and your thumb and then around to the front.

4 Bring the knitting needle, and the ball-end loop around it, through the loop of yarn on your thumb.

5 Slip the loop off your thumb. Pull gently on the tail end of the yarn to tighten the stitch.* You have cast on a second stitch.

6 Repeat from * until you have cast on the required number of stitches onto the needle.

cable cast on

This method of casting on uses two knitting needles and produces a neat, firm edge. Always make the slip knot about 15cm from the end of the yarn to leave a tail long enough to weave in when the knitting is complete (see page 125).

1 Hold the needle with the knot on in your left hand. From left to right, put the tip of the right-hand needle into the front of the knot.

2 *Wind the ball end of the yarn around the tip of the right-hand needle, going under and then over the top of the needle.

3 Bring the right-hand knitting needle, and the loop of yarn wound around the tip of it, through the slip knot.

4 Slip the loop of yarn on the right-hand needle onto the left-hand needle. Pull gently on the ball end of the yarn to tighten the stitch. You have cast on a second stitch.

5 For all the following stitches, put the right-hand needle between the two previous stitches, instead of through the last stitch.

6 Repeat from * until you have cast on the required number of stitches onto the needle.

knit stitch

This is the first and most basic stitch you need to learn to start knitting, and it is very similar to the cable cast on (see page 113). First cast on the number of stitches needed for the project using whichever cast on method the pattern asks for.

1 *From left to right, put the tip of the right-hand needle into the front of the next stitch on the left-hand needle.

2 Wind the working yarn around the tip of the right-hand needle, going under and then over the top of the needle.

3 Bring the right-hand needle, and the loop of yarn around it, through the stitch on the left-hand needle.

4 Keeping the loop on the right-hand needle, slip the original stitch off the left-hand needle. You have knitted a stitch. Repeat from * until you have knitted all the stitches on the left-hand needle. Then swap the needles in your hands and you are ready to begin the next row.

purl stitch

This is the other basic stitch used in knitting.

1 *From right to left, put the tip of the right-hand needle into the front of the next stitch on the left-hand needle.

2 From front to back, wind the working yarn over the tip of the right-hand needle.

3 Bring the right-hand needle, and the loop of yarn around it, through the stitch on the left-hand needle.

4 Keeping the loop on the right-hand needle, slip the original stitch off the left-hand needle. You have purled a stitch. Repeat from * until you have purled all the stitches on the left-hand needle. Then swap the needles in your hands and you are ready to begin the next row.

casting off

This is the way you finish off your knitting, securing the stitches so that they don't unravel. It is shown here on a knit row, but can be worked just as well on a purl row: simply purl the stitches instead of knitting them.

1 Knit the first two stitches on the left-hand needle.

2 *Put the tip of the left-hand needle into the first stitch you knitted and lift it over the second stitch. Drop this first stitch off both needles.

3 Knit another stitch and repeat from * to cast off all the stitches in turn.

4 When you have just one stitch left on the right-hand needle, pull gently to open it up a little and slip it off the needle. Cut the yarn 15cm from the knitting. Thread the cut end through the last stitch and pull gently on the cut end to tighten the stitch.

knitting in the round

This is the technique used to work seamless tubes of knitting. It might seem fiddly at first, but do persevere as it isn't difficult once you get the hang of manipulating the four needles. An advantage of working in the round is that you only have to knit rows – there are no purl rows – to make stocking stitch. You can more or less ignore the needles that you are not actually knitting with.

The principles employed in holding two needles and yarn (see page 111) also apply when knitting in the round on four needles. Bring the lower end of the needle holding the stitches being worked over the top of the end of the needle below to it to allow you to knit easily. You can safely ignore the two other needles holding stitches: as long as the stitches are not too close to either end of the needle, they shouldn't fall off.

1 Cast on the required number of stitches using the appropriate cast on method (see pages 112–113) and double-pointed needles. Unless the pattern says otherwise, distribute the stitches evenly between three needles. To do this, slip one-third of them off one end of the needle onto a second needle. Slip another third of them off the other end of the needle onto a third needle. If you push the stitches to the middle of each needle they shouldn't fall off.

2 Before you join the stitches into the round, slip a stitch marker onto the free end of one needle. Make sure that the row of stitches is lying in a straight line across the three needles; not twisted at all. Put the fourth needle through the first stitch you cast on. Wrap the working end of the yarn firmly around the tip of the fourth needle and knit the stitch, pulling it tight so that the three needles with stitches on form a triangle.

3 Continue knitting the stitches on the first needle. When they are all knitted, then that needle is free and becomes the spare needle with which you can knit the stitches on the second needle.

4 Just keep knitting the stitches off each needle in turn to create a knitted tube. When you reach the stitch marker, slip it onto the next needle so that you always know where the beginning of the round is. Knit the first stitch on each needle firmly, pulling the yarn tight, to prevent gaps appearing in the knitting where the needles 'join'. If they do start to appear, then knit one stitch off the next needle for a round to change the position of the 'joins'.

tension

The patterns in this book all specify the yarn you should use to knit them and the tension the project requires. This is the number of stitches and rows there are in 10 x 10cm of knitted fabric. It is important that you work to the tension the pattern states or the knitted fabric will be too baggy (if your tension is too loose), or too firm (if your tension is too tight). This might not sound dreadful, but it will affect the way your project looks and if your tension is too loose, you will use more yarn and may run out before finishing the knitting. So do take the time to knit a tension swatch before starting to make your favourite odd-bod character.

knitting a tension swatch

First, find the tension information given in the pattern. It will say something like: '22 stitches and 28 rows to 10cm square over stocking stitch using 4mm needles'. What this means it that, using the stated yarn and needles and working in the specified stitch pattern, in a piece of knitting 10cm by 10cm you must have 22 stitches in one direction and 28 rows in the other direction.

So, using the right yarn and needles, cast on the number of stitches stated, plus ten. Knit the number of rows stated – in the stitch pattern specified – plus ten, then cast off. Make the cast off as loose as you can to avoid pulling in the top edge of the knitting.

measuring your tension

The next step is to accurately measure your tension. Do this a few stitches or rows in from the edges as the cast on and cast off edges and the row ends can be tighter or looser than the stitches in the middle of the knitting, which are the ones that you must count.

Lay the swatch flat without stretching it. To count the number of stitches, lay a ruler across the swatch so that 10cm is measured out a few stitches in from either edge. Put a knitter's pin into the swatch at either end of the measured distance. Remove the ruler and count the number of stitches between the pins.

To count the number of rows, repeat the process, but lay the ruler vertically on the swatch so that 10cm is measured out a few rows from either edge.

altering your tension

If you have the same numbers of stitches and rows as stated in the pattern, then you have the correct tension. You can go ahead and knit the project that you have chosen.

However, if you do not have the right numbers of stitches and rows, you need to alter your tension. Do not do this by trying to knit more tightly or loosely. Everyone has a 'natural' tension, the tension they automatically knit to, and if you try to knit to a different tension your stitches will be uneven. Also, you will usually forget that you are trying to knit more tightly and your natural tension will reassert itself, then you are back to square one.

The way to alter your tension is to change the size of the knitting needles you are using. If you have too few stitches and rows, knit the swatch again using needles one size smaller. So, if the pattern asks for 5mm needles, try again using 4.5mm needles.

If you have too many stitches and rows, then try again with needles one size larger: 5.5mm needles instead of 5mm.

This may sound time-consuming and frustrating, but it's much better to knit a little square a few times than to spend more time and effort knitting a whole project that doesn't look right.

measuring stitches   **measuring rows**

increases

Increasing is making extra stitches in a row to make the knitting wider or to shape it.

make one (M1) This method involves creating a brand new stitch between two existing ones. It is almost completely invisible in the finished knitting.

1 Knit to the position of the increase. Using the tip of the left-hand needle, pick up the loop of yarn lying between the next two stitches. Pick it up by putting the tip of the needle through the front of the loop.

2 Knit into the back of the picked-up loop on the left-hand needle, then drop the loop.
You have created a completely new stitch and so increased by one stitch. The principle is exactly the same on a purl row.

increase (inc) This method involves knitting twice into a stitch. The increase is visible in the finished knitting as the second stitch made – which will lie to the right of the original stitch – has a small bar of yarn across the bottom of it.

1 Knit to the position of the increase. Knit into the next stitch in the usual way (see page 114), but do not drop the original stitch off the left-hand needle.

2 Now knit into the back of the same stitch on the left-hand needle, then drop it off the needle. You have made two stitches out of one and so increased by one stitch. The principle is exactly the same on a purl row.

make one left and right

You will find that some projects in this book specify 'M1L' (make one left) and 'M1R' (make one right). This is because, depending on which method you use, the made stitch slopes to the right or to the left. The technique shown here is 'M1L'. To work 'M1R', pick up the strand between the two stitches by putting the tip of the left-hand needle through the back of the loop. Then knit into the front of the picked-up loop. If the project simply specifies 'M1', then you can use whichever of the two methods of making a stitch that you find easiest.

reverse shaping

When reverse shaping, it is important to use the knit or purl increase or decrease that will follow the direction in which the shape of the creature is developing. On shaping rows, reverse the stitch (knit for purl or vice versa) and then use the table below to check which increase or decrease should be used at the beginning and end of the row to achieve a smooth effect. The direction the stitches slope in is given as though you are looking at them from the knit side of the work.

Knit increase

Beginning of row	End of row
M1R (right slanting)	M1L (left slanting)

Knit decrease

Beginning of row	End of row
skpo (left slanting)	k2tog (right slanting)

Purl increase

Beginning of row	End of row
M1L (left slanting)	M1R (right slanting)

Purl decrease

Beginning of row	End of row
p2tog (right slanting)	p2togtbl (left slanting)

decreases

Decreasing involves taking away stitches in a row to make the knitting narrower. Decreases slant in different directions, so when used at either end of a row, they mirror each other.

knit two together (k2tog) In this method you knit two stitches together to make one. The decrease slants to the right on a knit row.

purl two together (p2tog) This uses the same principle as k2tog to decrease stitches on a purl row. The decrease slants to the left on a purl row.

Knit to the position of the decrease. From left to right, put the tip of the right-hand needle through the front of the second stitch from the end of the left-hand needle, then through the first one. Knit the two stitches together in the usual way, just as if they were one.
You have made two stitches into one and so decreased by one stitch.

Purl to the position of the decrease. From right to left, put the tip of the right-hand needle through the next two stitches on the left-hand needle. Purl the two stitches together in the usual way, just as if they were one.
You have made two stitches into one and so decreased by one stitch.

slip one, knit one pass slipped stitch over (skpo) This method involves slipping a stitch and then passing the next one over it, rather like casting off. This decrease slants to the left on a knit row.

1 Knit to the position of the decrease. Put the right-hand needle into the next stitch, as if you were going to knit it, but slip it from the left-hand to the right-hand needle without knitting it.

2 Knit the next stitch on the left-hand needle in the usual way.

3 Put the tip of the left-hand needle into the slipped stitch and lift it over the knitted stitch, then drop it off both needles.
You have decreased by one stitch.

through the back loop (tbl)

Knitting or purling a stitch through the back of the loop (rather than through the front as normal), twists the stitch. This is used mainly in shaping to change the direction an increase or decrease slants in. For example, 'k2togtbl' means knit two together (see page 119), but through the back loops.

To knit a stitch through the back loop, put the right-hand needle from right to left through the stitch, but putting it behind the left-hand needle. Take the yarn around the tip of the right-hand needle in the usual way and knit the stitch.

To purl a stitch through the back loop, put the right-hand needle from left to right through the back of the stitch: when you straighten the left-hand needle the stitch will be twisted around it, as shown. Take the yarn around the tip of the right-hand needle in the usual way and purl the stitch.

slipping stitches

Slipped stitches can be worked knitwise or purlwise. If the pattern does not specify which way to slip a stitch, slip it knitwise on a knit row and purlwise on a purl row.

pick up and knit

Use this technique to start knitting from the edge of a piece that has been cast off. The knitting pattern will tell you how many stitches to pick up from where.

1 On a knit row, slip a stitch knitwise by putting the right-hand needle into the next stitch, as if to knit it, but slip it onto the needle without actually knitting it. Knit the next stitch in the usual way.

2 The principle is the same if you are slipping a stitch purlwise. Put the right-hand needle into the next stitch, as if to purl it, but slip it onto the needle without actually purling it. Purl the next stitch in the usual way.

1 Hold the yarn with which you are going to pick up the new stitches at the back of the finished piece. Put a knitting needle through the middle of the stitch to be picked up from. At the back, loop the yarn over the tip of the needle.

2 Bring the needle back through the stitch, bringing the loop of yarn through with it. You have picked up one stitch.

short-row shaping

This is a technique for creating curved pieces of knitting. Each row will tell you to knit a number of stitches, then 'short-row-wrap the next st, turn'. Follow these wrapping techniques to wrap the next stitch in the row, then turn the knitting by swapping the needles in your hands.

on a knit row Knit the number of stitches stated then wrap the next stitch as follows.

1 Slip the next stitch on the left-hand needle purlwise onto the right-hand needle (see page 120).

2 Bring the yarn forward between the tips of the needles.

3 Now slip the stitch back onto the left-hand needle, then take the yarn to the back again, thus wrapping it around the slipped stitch. Here, the yarn is shown as a loop so that you can see what is happening, but you must pull it taut. Now you are ready to turn the work and purl the next row.

on a purl row Purl the number of stitches stated then wrap the next stitch as follows.

1 Slip the next stitch on the left-hand needle purlwise onto the right-hand needle (see page 120).

2 Take the yarn back between the tips of the needles.

3 Now slip the stitch back onto the left-hand needle, then bring the yarn to the front between the needles again, thus wrapping it around the slipped stitch. Now you are ready to turn the work and knit the next row.

picking up wraps on a knit row
Once the shaping rows are completed, you will knit or purl across all the stitches in the row. When doing this it is essential to work the wrap loops together with the slipped stitches they encircle to prevent holes forming. Follow the technique shown on each wrapped stitch as you get to it.

From the front and using the tip of the right-hand needle, pick up the wrap loop around the base of the slipped stitch. Slip this loop onto the tip of the left-hand needle and then knit the loop and stitch together as if they were one. The loop will not be visible on the right side of the work.

picking up wraps on a purl row
Working across the knitting on a purl row, follow the technique shown on each wrapped stitch as you get to it.

From behind and using the tip of the right-hand needle, pick up the wrap loop around the base of the slipped stitch. Slip this loop onto the tip of the left-hand needle then purl the loop and stitch together as one. The loop will not be visible on the right side of the work.

colour knitting

There are two main techniques for colour knitting, Fair Isle and intarsia. For both techniques it is important to twist the yarns around one another as shown to prevent holes appearing between the different-coloured yarns. Whether colours change in straight lines or on the diagonal will, of course, depend on the motif you are knitting. Shown here are the principles of making all the colour changes.

fair isle This method strands yarn across the back of the work and is used to knit continuous patterns. When using this technique, do not pull the yarn tight across the back of the work or it will pucker up. However, stranding it too loosely will result in loops on the back and baggy stitches, so practise the technique to get the balance right before starting a project.

1 On a knit row, knit to the first colour change. Bring the new colour yarn (purple) from under the original colour yarn (pink) and then around the needle to knit the stitch.

2 Knit the stitches in the new colour yarn. When you get to the next colour change, bring that yarn (pink) from under the new colour yarn (purple) and around the needle to knit the stitch.

3 If the interval between colour changes is more than three stitches, you will need to weave the yarn not in use into the back of a stitch to prevent long loops forming on the back. Bring the working yarn under the yarn not in use, then knit the next stitch in the working yarn. Here the purple yarn is being woven in to the back of a pink stitch.

4 On a purl row, purl to the first colour change. Bring the new colour yarn (purple) under the original colour (pink) and then around the needle to purl the stitch.

5 At the next colour change, bring the original yarn (here it is pink) over the new yarn (purple) and purl the stitch.

6 If the interval between colour changes is more than three stitches you must also weave in the yarn not in use on purl rows. Use the same procedure as for knit rows.

Above: where the yarn not in use is woven into the back of a stitch it may well show a little on the front, either as a slight pucker in the stitch or as a spot of colour between stitches. This is inherent in Fair Isle knitting.

intarsia This method uses a separate ball of yarn for each coloured area. To avoid tangling the yarns, wind long lengths onto bobbins and knit from these.

1 On a knit row, knit to the first colour change. Bring the new colour yarn (magenta) over the original colour yarn (blue) and then around the needle to knit the stitch.

2 Knit the stitches in the new colour yarn. When you get to the next colour change, bring that yarn (magenta) over the original colour yarn (blue) and around the needle to knit the stitch. To knit the next stitch in blue on the row shown, bring the blue yarn over the magenta yarn: this is shown below on a purl row where it can be seen more easily.

3 On a purl row, purl to the first colour change. Bring the new colour yarn (magenta) under the original colour yarn (blue) and then around the needle to purl the stitch.

4 Purl the stitches in the new colour yarn. When you get to the next colour change, bring that yarn (magenta) under the original colour yarn (blue) and around the needle to knit the stitch.

5 To work the next colour change, bring the new colour (now blue) over the old colour (magenta) on both knit and purl rows.

Above: Weaving in ends neatly (see page 125) gives you the opportunity to tighten up any loose stitches at the beginning and end of an intarsia colour motif.

cables

Cabling simply involves swapping the positions on the needle of groups of stitches. Shown here is cable four but you can cable two, six or eight stitches just as easily.

cable four back (C4B) A back cable twists to the right on the right side of the work.

1 Purl to the position of the cable. Take the yarn between the tips of the needles to the back of the work.

2 Slip the next two stitches on the left-hand knitting needle onto a cable needle.

3 With the cable needle at the back of the work, knit the next two stitches on the left-hand needle. Just ignore the cable needle while doing this.

4 Now knit the two stitches on the cable needle. Slide them to the end of the needle and knit them in the usual way. Purl to the end of the row, or to the next cable.

cable four front (C4F) A front (or 'forward', as it is also known) cable twists to the left on the right side of the work. Work it in a similar way to a front cable, but leave the cable needle at the front of the work instead of at the back while you knit the next two stitches on the left-hand needle.

Left: this swatch of C4B is worked over eight rows; that is to say, the cable is twisted on every eighth row of knitting.

embroidering faces

This where you give your creature its personality. Each project tells you how the creature shown was embroidered, but you can change them as you wish.

Satin stitch

Backstitch

For instance, Angry Ginger (page 54) looks angry because he has frowning eyebrows and spiky teeth, but you could make him happy or hopeful by turning his eyebrows the other way up and giving him a smile. After you have knitted and stuffed your creature you are ready to embroider the face. You can use tapestry yarn in the colours you want, or use up any scraps of lightweight knitting yarn you might have lying around. Use a large embroidery needle with a big hole so you can thread your chosen yarn through it easily. The stitches and rows of the knitted fabric provide a natural grid, so it is easy to stitch onto.

Start by coming through from the back of the creature, guiding the needle to where you want the first eye to be on the front – you can snip off the tail of yarn later. Make a small backstitch to secure the yarn then backstitch the outline of the eye as if you were drawing it: I use a stitch about 5mm long. After you have stitched the outline, fill in the whites and coloured irises with satin stitch. Secure the yarn with a small backstitch, take it back through the creature and cut off the tail on the back.
Embroider other features, such as mouths and cheeks, in the same way, outlining the shape first and then filling it in if necessary.

using a stitch holder

Some patterns tell you to place a certain number of stitches on a holder. You will work the remaining stitches on the knitting needles, then come back to the stitches on the holder and work those.

joining in new yarn

When you reach the end of a ball of yarn you need to join in a new one to continue knitting. You also use this method to join in a different-coloured yarn in colour knitting (see pages 122–123).

weaving in ends

When you have finished your knitting, you need to weave in any ends left dangling from casting on, casting off and joining in new yarn.

Simply slip the required number of stitches from the needle onto the holder. Make sure that the holder is securely closed, then ignore it until the pattern tells you otherwise. At that point, slip the stitches back onto the needle and work them as instructed.

If you are joining in new yarn because you have come to the end of a ball, join it in at the end of a row. You must have a length of yarn approximately four times the width of the knitting to knit one row.

Tie the new yarn in a loose single knot around the tail end of the old yarn. Slide the knot up to the work and pull it tight. Leave a 15cm tail of each yarn to weave in later.

Thread a knitter's sewing needle with the tail of yarn. Take the needle back and forth, not in and over, through the backs of several stitches. Go through approximately four stitches in one direction, then work back through the last two again. If you are weaving in ends from colour knitting, weave the tails into stitches of the same colour to stop them showing on the front.

blocking

Once you have finished your knitting project, it will benefit from being blocked. This smooths out the fabric, helps hide any small imperfections and makes the project much easier to sew up.

On an ironing board, lay out your project pieces without stretching them. Ease each piece to the correct size and shape. Pin the pieces to the board by pushing dressmaker's pins through the edge stitches into the board.

Carefully following the instructions on the yarn ball band, press all the pieces. Leave them pinned out until they are completely cold. Then take out all the pins and you are ready to start sewing up your project.

sewing up

Many people rush this stage of making a knitting project, which is a mistake. Take your time, use mattress stitch as shown here, and your seams will be smooth and neat, giving your knitting a professional finish. Use the yarn you used to knit the project to sew it up, though if the yarn is very fine or breaks easily, use a stronger one in the same fibre and colour.

1 Thread a knitter's sewing needle with a long length of yarn. Here, a contrast colour has been used for clarity. Secure the yarn on the back of one of the pieces to be joined by taking it over a couple of stitches, a couple of times. Bring the needle to the front of the fabric, bringing it up between the first two stitches on the first row.

2 Right-side up, lay the other project piece to be joined next to the first piece. From the front, take the needle through the fabric between the first two stitches on the first row and up under the bars of two stitches. Pull the yarn through.

3 Take the needle back through where it came out on the first piece and up under the bars of two stitches. Take the needle back to the other piece, through where it came out and up under the bars of two stitches. Zigzag between the pieces, taking the needle under two stitch bars each time. Gently pull the yarn to close the seam as you work.

Above: worked neatly a mattress stitched seam blends in to the knitted fabric.

abbreviations

Here is a list of the abbreviations you will find in the knitting patterns in this book.

A, B, C, etc	colours as indicated in the pattern	**double-inc**	knit into the front, back and front again of the same stitch	**p**	purl	**skpo**	slip one, knit one, pass slipped stitch over
alt	alternate			**patt(s)**	pattern(s)	**sl**	slip
approx	approximate	**dpn**	double-pointed needle(s)	**PB**	place bead	**st(s)**	stitch(es)
beg	begin, beginning, begins	**g**	gram(s)	**psso**	pass slipped stitch over	**st st**	stocking stitch
C4B	cable four (or number stated) back	**inc(s)**	increase, increasing, increases	**rem**	remain, remaining	**tbl**	through the back loop
				rep(s)	repeat(s)	**tog**	together
C4F	cable four (or number stated) forward	**k2tog**	knit two together	**rev st st**	reverse stocking stitch	**WS**	wrong side
		k	knit	**RS**	right side	*****	repeat instructions between/following * as many times as instructed
cm	centimetre(s)	**m**	metre(s)	**s2tog, k1, psso**	slip next two stitches together knitwise (put needle into second then first stitch to do this), knit next stitch, pass slipped stitches over knitted stitch		
cont	continue	**mm**	millimetres			**[ ]**	repeat instructions between [ ] as many times as instructed
dec(s)	decrease, decreasing, decreases	**M1**	make one stitch				
		M1L	make one stitch left				
DK	double knitting	**M1R**	make one stitch right				
		p2tog	purl two together				

yarn information

Here is the fibre content and meterage for all the yarns used in this book.

Debbie Bliss Baby Cashmerino 50g; 125m; 55% merino wool, 33% microfibre, 12% cashmere.

Debbie Bliss Cashmerino DK 50g; 110m; 55% merino wool, 33% mircofibre, 12% cashmere.

Debbie Bliss Donegal Luxury Tweed 50g; 88m; 85% wool, 15% angora.

Debbie Bliss Prima 50g; 100m; 80% bamboo, 20% merino wool.

Debbie Bliss Rialto 50g; 105m; 100% extra fine merino wool.

Lang Yarns West 50g; 92m; 55% new wool, 45% acrylic.

Lion Brand Cotton-Ease 100g; 188m; 50% cotton, 50% acrylic.

Lion Brand Fishermen's Wool 227g; 425m; 100% pure virgin wool.

Lion Brand Sock-Ease 100g; 400m; 75% wool, 25% nylon.

Lion Brand Vanna's Choice Baby 100g; 156m; 100% acrylic.

Rowan 4ply Soft 50g; 175m; 100% merino wool.

Rowan All Seasons Cotton 50g; 90m; 60% cotton, 40% acrylic/ microfibre.

Rowan Cashcotton 4ply 50g; 180m; 35% cotton, 25% polyamide, 18% viscose, 9% cashmere.

Rowan Cotton Glacé 50g; 115m; 100% cotton.

Rowan Kid Classic 50g; 140m; 70% lambswool, 26% mohair, 4% nylon.

Rowan Kidsilk Haze 25g; 210m; 70% super kid mohair, 30% silk.

Rowan Pure Wool 4ply 50g; 160m; 100% super wash wool.

Rowan Pure Wool DK 50g; 125m; 100% super wash wool.

Rowan Scottish Tweed 4ply 25g; 110m; 100% pure new wool.

Rowan Wool Cotton 50g; 113m; 50% merino wool, 50% cotton.

Sublime Angora Merino 50g; 120m; 80% extra fine merino wool, 20% angora.

Sublime Cashmerino Silk DK 50g; 116m; 75% extra fine merino wool, 20% silk, 5% cashmere.

Twilley's Washable Goldfingering 25g; 95m; 80% viscose, 20% polyester,

substituting yarn

If you decide to use a yarn that is different to the one suggested, follow these simple rules before buying.

Firstly, unless you are an experienced knitter do use a yarn that is the suggested weight. If you use a DK-weight where the project asks for a chunky weight, you may have problems with some of the patterns.

Secondly, it is the number of metres of yarn in each ball, not the weight of the ball, that is important. Balls of different brands of yarn, even if they are the same weight, will not necessarily contain the same number of metres of yarn. So you cannot just buy the number of balls the pattern asks for in your substitute yarn: you need to do two sums, but they are simple ones. Given on the left are the number of metres per ball for the yarns used in the projects. Multiply the appropriate number of metres by the number of balls needed to knit the project. This will give you the total number of metres of yarn you will need.

Now check the ball band of your substitute yarn to see how many metres there are in a ball. Divide the total number of metres needed by the number in one ball of the substitute yarn and this will tell you how many balls of that yarn you need to buy.

Before you start knitting the project, you absolutely must knit a tension swatch in the substitute yarn to check that it will achieve the tension stated in the pattern.

needle sizes

Knitting needles are sold in standard sizes, though there are three different measuring systems. This chart compares sizes across all three systems.

metric	US	old UK and Canadian
25	50	–
19	35	
15	19	–
10	15	000
9	13	00
8	11	0
7.50	11	1
7	10½	2
6.50	10½	3
6	10	4
5.50	9	5
5	8	6
4.50	7	7
4	6	8
3.75	5	9
3.50	4	–
3.25	3	10
3	2/3	11
2.75	2	12
2.25	1	13
2	0	14

Conversions

Metric	Imperial
5mm	$1/4$in
7mm	$1/4$in
10mm	$1/2$in
12mm	$1/2$in
15mm	$1/2$in
17mm	$3/4$in
20mm	$3/4$in
30mm	1in
35mm	$1^1/2$in
1cm	$1/2$in
1.5cm	$1/2$in
2cm	$3/4$in
2.5cm	1in
3cm	1in
3.5cm	$1^1/2$in
4cm	$1^1/2$in
5cm	2in
6cm	$2^1/4$in
6.5cm	$2^1/2$in
7cm	$2^3/4$in
8cm	3in
9cm	$3^1/2$in
9.5cm	$3^3/4$in
10cm	4in
11cm	$4^1/2$in
12cm	$4^3/4$in
12.5cm	5in
13cm	5in
14cm	$5^1/2$in
15cm	6in
16cm	$6^1/2$in
17cm	7in
18cm	7in
20cm	8in
22cm	9in
25cm	10in
26cm	$10^1/2$in
28cm	$11^1/4$in
30cm	12in

Resources

UK

Debbie Bliss yarns
Designer Yarns Ltd
Units 8–10
Newbridge Industrial Estate
Pitt Street
Keighley
West Yorkshire BD21 4PQ
Tel: 01535 664222
www.designeryarns.uk.com

Lang Yarns
Artyarn
10 High Street
Pointon
Sleaford
Lincolnshire NG34 0LX
Tel: 01529 240510
www.artyarn.co.uk

Lion Brand Yarn
www.banyantreeyarns.com

Rowan Yarns
Green Lane Mill
Holmfirth
West Yorkshire HD9 2DX
Tel: 01484 681881
www.knitrowan.com

Sublime yarns
Tel: 01924 369666
www.sublimeyarns.com

Twilleys of Stamford
www.twilleys.co.uk for stockists

USA

Debbie Bliss yarns
Sublime yarns
Knitting Fever Inc.
P.O. Box 502
Roosevelt
New York 11575
Tel: (516) 546 3600
www.knittingfever.com

Lang Yarns
Berroco Inc.
P.O. Box 367
14 Elmdale Road
Uxbridge, MA 01569
Tel: (508) 278 25 27
www.berroco.com

Lion Brand Yarn
135 Kero Road
Carlstadt, NJ 07072
Tel: 1 800 258 9276
www.lionbrand.com

Rowan Yarns
Westminster Fibers Inc.
4 Townsend West
Suite 8
Nashua, NH 03063
Tel: (063) 886 5041
www.westminsterfibers.com

Twilleys of Stamford
www.twilleys.co.uk for stockists

Canada

Debbie Bliss yarns
Rowan Yarns
Sublime yarns
Diamond Yarns Ltd
155 Martin Ross Avenue
Unit 3
Toronto
Ontario M3J 2L9
Tel: (416) 736 6111
www.diamondyarn.com

Lang Yarns
Estelle Design & Sales Limited
Units 65/67
2220 Midland Avenue
Scarborough
Ontario M1P 3E6
Tel: 1 800 387 5167
www.estelledesigns.ca

Lion Brand Yarn
www.lionbrand.com for stockists

Twilleys of Stamford
www.twilleys.co.uk for stockists

Donna Wilson can be contacted at info@donnawilson.com. Visit her website at donnawilson.com.

Acknowledgements

I would like to thank Luise and Kate for being such amazing knitters and helping me interpret the creatures into hand knits so fantastically. Thanks to Tamar, Karin, Rachel and Vanessa for their help and Jon for all his support. Thanks also to Cindy and the team at CICO Books for commissioning this book, to Luis for his creative book design and to Marilyn for diligent pattern checking. Rowan Yarns, Debbie Bliss and Lion Brand were all very generous in supplying great yarns for the book.